TRANSLATING TRUTH

foreword by J. I. PACKER

TRANSLATING
TRUTH

The Case for Essentially Literal Bible Translation

WAYNE GRUDEM · LELAND RYKEN · C. JOHN COLLINS
VERN S. POYTHRESS · BRUCE WINTER

CROSSWAY BOOKS

A PUBLISHING MINISTRY OF
GOOD NEWS PUBLISHERS
WHEATON, ILLINOIS

Translating Truth: The Case for Essentially Literal Bible Translation

Copyright © 2005 by Crossway Books, a publishing ministry of Good News Publishers

Published by Crossway Books
   a publishing ministry of Good News Publishers
   1300 Crescent Street
   Wheaton, Illinois 60187

Cover design: Jon McGrath

Cover photo: Getty Images

First printing 2005

Printed in the United States of America

Library of Congress Cataloging-in-Publication Data

Translating truth : the case for essentially literal Bible translation /
C. John Collins, Wayne Grudem, Vern Sheridan Poythress, Leland
Ryken, and Bruce Winter; foreword by J. I. Packer
  p. cm.
  Includes bibliographical references and index.
  ISBN 13: 978-1-58134-755-5
  ISBN 10: 1-58134-755-3 (tpb)
  1. Bible—Translating. 2. Bible—Inspiration.
BS449.T748 2005
220.501—dc22   2005024571

VP		16	15	14	13	12	11	10	09	08	07	06
16	15	14	13	12	11	10	9	8	7	6	5	4	3	2

CONTENTS

PUBLISHER'S NOTE

THE ESSAYS INCLUDED in this volume were first presented as papers at the annual meeting of the Evangelical Theological Society in November 2004. The purpose of publishing these papers now as a collection is to encourage the ongoing, careful reflection on methodology and issues in Bible translation—that necessary work, which the Christian church is called to undertake, with fear and trembling before our sovereign, holy God, for the sake of the gospel and the truth of God's Word.

We are grateful for the insights expressed in this volume on a variety of issues and from a number of perspectives. Each of the contributors was part of the fourteen-member Translation Oversight Committee for the English Standard Version (ESV) Bible, published in 2001.* We are likewise grateful to Dr. J. I. Packer, who served as General Editor for the ESV Bible, for his foreword to this volume, which provides a very helpful framework for understanding and carrying forward the discussion.

The words of the Bible are the very words of God, and so the work of translating these words is of utmost importance, with eternal consequences. As Jesus said, "Man shall not live by bread alone, but by every word that comes from the mouth of God" (Matt. 4:4); or as Peter confessed, "Lord, to whom shall we go? You have the words of eternal life" (John 6:68). The work of Bible translation may be undertaken only with fear and trembling and abject dependence on our sovereign, holy Lord, with the understanding (as noted in the preface to the ESV Bible) that, "We know that no Bible translation is perfect or final; but we also know that God uses imperfect and inadequate things to his honor and praise.

---

*For further information about the English Standard Version (ESV) Bible, please visit the ESV website at esvbible.org.

So to our triune God and to his people we offer what we have done, with our prayers that it may prove useful, with gratitude for much help given, and with ongoing wonder that our God should ever have entrusted to us so momentous a task."

Soli Deo Gloria!—To God alone be the glory!

—Lane T. Dennis, Ph.D.
President and Publisher

FOREWORD

IT IS ONE OF THE glories of God's grace to a sinful world that he constantly speaks in and through Holy Scripture to Christian minds and hearts, as the Holy Spirit illuminates the ancient words and applies their message to us to meet new situations and needs. Digging into Scripture, therefore, is one of the most life-giving things believers ever do.

Evangelical Christians have always known this, and Bible study (meaning careful, prayerful, thoughtful reading and rereading of the text, with or without the help of books and notes) has always been the central feature of evangelical private devotion. The mainstream church's Trinitarian, incarnational, historical-redemptive understanding of biblical faith—the only understanding, in fact, that the canonical corpus will yield—has been the interpretative base for this searching of the Scriptures from the start. For most of the nineteenth century, following the Evangelical Revival in Britain and the two Great Awakenings in America, the religion of the Protestant churches both sides of the Atlantic was essentially evangelical; the historic faith was faithfully taught by preaching, catechizing, and distribution of literature, and diligent reading of the King James Version both privately and in the family was a fixed point in Christian discipleship.

In those days, Christianity was strong. But in the twentieth century both the ministry of teaching biblical truth and biblical living and the discipline of feeding on the Bible at home crumbled away. As uncertainty about the contents of the Bible grew through the skepticism and revisionism of liberal scholarship, so interest in the Bible declined throughout the Western world. Today, adult members of churches in most cases have never been taught the Christian faith by anybody, and the Bible is to them a closed book—or, should they perchance dip into it, a bewilderment from start to finish. Back in Britain, almost two generations ago, I heard it declared that the minister's first priority is to teach, and his second priority is to teach, and his third priority is to teach. More than fifty years of not doing this have inevitably hastened the decline of interest in the Bible and in effect promoted the sense of its irrelevance to modern life.

Facing this pervasive shrinkage of Bible knowledge and influence, many in the churches hoped that simplifying and streamlining public worship would bring people back to the life of devotion and that simplified and streamlined versions of Holy Scripture would bring people back to the habit of Bible reading. Neither hope has been fulfilled in today's post-Christian West, nor seems likely to be. But both programs have been zealously pursued, and as a result the English-speaking world has before it not only the kaleidoscope of "blended worship" but also more translations of the Bible than this or any other language group has ever had. Surveying the translations produced within the past sixty years, we find that they fall into three categories, the third of which is an extension of the second.

The usual label for the first category is "word-for-word" or "essentially literal" translations. Understanding translation as the discipline of tuning in to writers of other times and other cultures, as well as of other languages, these versions aim to be as transparent as possible to the vocabulary, sentence structure, thought process, literary purpose, situational context, personal style, rhetorical strategy, and communicatory technique of each Bible author, within the limits that good English allows. This was the path traveled by William Tyndale and the King James Version (both with what by today's standards was some license); and it is the path that is now traveled by the Revised Standard Version (with much literary skill but some academically inspired blurring), the New King James Version and the New American Standard Version (both with greater accuracy, but less literary grace), and by the English Standard Version, with the New Revised Standard Version, the New English Translation, and the Holman Christian Standard Version not far behind.

These versions are not, of course, word-for-word in any mechanical sense; they seek simply to catch all the meaning that the text expresses, book by book, section by section, paragraph by paragraph, and sentence by sentence, in a way that the original writer, were he with us today, would recognize as a full and exact rendering of what he sought to put across to his own readership, now expressed in clusters of English words that as far as possible match those that he used himself. Translations of this type require the reader to learn what he can about the ancient and in some ways alien culture in which the text is steeped, knowing that he will miss some of the meaning unless he does so. Plainly, these versions will yield their richest rewards when linked with the helps of an ongoing expository ministry in the pulpit, a commentary and Bible dictionary handy at home, and a heart passionate to know God.

The second category is usually labeled "thought-for-thought" or "dynamic equivalent" renderings. Here the translators' avowed aim is to induce, directly and immediately, the same positive complex of compelling interest and intellectual, emotional, and volitional response that the original writers sought to trigger in their own readership, and the developed method is to modify the wording and imagery of the text as a means to this end. Lively English covering the semantic field of the original in a consistently colloquial way, bringing out its implications without being bound by its sentence structure, is the goal. Examples are the Good News Bible, the Living Bible and the New Living Translation (the latter a skillful, scholarly recasting of the former), the Contemporary English Version, the New Century Bible, and God's Word. All are beamed first and foremost on adolescents and young adults who, so it is hoped, may be newly drawn into Bible reading by the brisk, vivid, even chummy way that everything is expressed.

The problem areas along this path are obvious. They all arise from the fact that what is being offered as a translation is trying to be an interpretative, evocative, applicatory paraphrase as well. To want to induce as clear an awareness as possible that the Bible story is the first part of our own story because the God of the Bible is God for us too is right, but a price has to be paid for this wholesale streamlining of Scripture. The danger is that by trying to be more than a translation, each "dynamic equivalent" version becomes less than a translation, in at least the following ways.

First, *focus is blurred*. Where the exact meaning of the text is elusive and more than one understanding is possible, this method requires a smooth rendering of the translators' views that will leave readers unaware that any difficulty and range of options exists at all. When the text contains technical terms (and there are many such in both

Testaments), the ideal of verbal informality will lead to an obscuring of their presence. (Example: "the righteousness of God" is a key technical phrase in Paul, most notably in Romans, but it does not appear in any of the dynamic equivalent versions that I mentioned, being paraphrased out every time.) If translating means expressing in another language the full meaning and character of the original as exactly as possible, this is under-translating.

Second, *fidelity is restricted*. When it is thought that a literal rendering would not be at once fully lucid to the casual reader, this method requires the substituting of present-day word pictures that may convey equivalent meaning with the same tone and thrust as the original had. But the reader, of course, will never know where this has been done or what it was that was changed, and evidently it is assumed that that does not matter. Does it not? When missionaries translating the New Testament for Arctic-dwellers designated the Lord Jesus Christ "the seal of God," because their intended readers did not know what a lamb was, perhaps it did not matter, and perhaps it was the best that could be done. Whether that is so when the original is intelligible and the change is only for warmth and chattiness is, however, more doubtful. Example: the Hebrew of Ecclesiastes 9:8 translates as, "Let your garments be always white. Let not oil be lacking on your head" (ESV). The New Living Translation reads, "Wear fine clothes, with a dash of cologne!" The point being made is, enjoy life's God-given enjoyments to the full. Is this change justified by the gain it brings in understanding? If the Hebrew words are not just the human writer's choice but God's own choice for communicating with us through what his penmen wrote, are changes of this kind justified at all? One begins to imagine wordsmiths like Ecclesiastes himself, and Isaiah, and Paul, looking down from heaven at our array of translations, and groaning again and again, "But that's not what I *wrote!*" If translation means serving authors by making what they wrote fully available in other languages (and surely Bible translation, whatever more it is, is at least that), what is being done here is under-translating.

Third, *foreshortening is imposed*—cultural foreshortening, that is. Colloquial paraphrase, however dynamically equivalent, cannot but preempt recognition of the cultural gap between the Bible worlds (there are several: Egyptian, Palestinian before and after the Exile, Persian, Greco-

Roman are the main ones) and our own world of today. This is very obvious in relation to the dash of cologne in the example we have just considered. Distancing (that is, discerning the differences between our world and worlds of the past) must precede assimilation (identifying transcendent similarities that reach above and beyond the differences). Cutting corners here, in rendering literature from the past—the Judeo-Christian past no less than any other—is always under-translating.

The third category of latter-day translations may be called exposition-for-text, or expanded paraphrase, renderings. These elaborate and amplify what is found in the semantic field of each text and passage, just as a pulpit expositor might do. The best-known examples are both one-man efforts: J. B. Phillips's *The New Testament in Modern English* and Eugene Peterson's *The Message*. The danger with them, obviously, is that they may read into the text more than is actually there—a lapse for which the fitting name would be over-translating.

In the essays that follow the weaknesses and limitations of some latter-day versions are bracingly highlighted. Let it be said that no one is implying that any type of dynamic equivalent rendering is useless. Even if the hope that a retranslated Bible could create for itself a new readership outside the church proves to be a pipe dream, many in churches where Bible study was no big thing will testify that the easy-flowing modern idiom of this or that new version has made Scripture accessible to them, and has shown them its relevance for them, in quite a new way. The true verdict seems to be that for beginners in Bible exploration and study, the merits of the best dynamic equivalent versions outweigh their real limitations. But for lifelong personal reading, with meditation and memorization, just as for public reading and pulpit exposition in church, the better option will unquestionably be one of the essentially literal translations; and I hope I may without offense mention here the English Standard Version, which was deliberately crafted to fulfill all these purposes together and, I believe, does so.

—J. I. Packer

CONTRIBUTORS

C. John Collins is Professor of Old Testament at Covenant Theological Seminary in St. Louis, where he teaches courses on Hebrew and Greek grammar and exegesis as well as Science and Theology. He has published numerous articles in technical journals as well as in *The New International Dictionary of Old Testament Theology and Exegesis*. He is the author of *The God of Miracles* and *Science and Faith: Friends or Foes?* (both Crossway), and of *Genesis 1–4: A Linguistic, Literary, and Theological Commentary* (Presbyterian & Reformed, forthcoming).

Wayne Grudem is Research Professor of Bible and Theology at Phoenix Seminary in Scottsdale, Arizona. He taught for twenty years at Trinity Evangelical Divinity School, where he was chairman of the department of Biblical and Systematic Theology. He has published twelve books, including *Systematic Theology* (Zondervan), *Recovering Biblical Manhood and Womanhood* (coedited with John Piper, Crossway), *The TNIV and the Gender-Neutral Bible Controversy* (coauthored with Vern Poythress, Broadman & Holman), *Evangelical Feminism and Biblical Truth* (Multnomah), and *The Gift of Prophecy in the New Testament and Today* (Crossway).

Vern S. Poythress is Professor of New Testament Interpretation at Westminster Theological Seminary in Philadelphia, where he has taught for more than twenty-five years. He is author of *Philosophy, Science and the Sovereignty of God* (Presbyterian & Reformed); *Symphonic Theology* (Zondervan); *Science and Hermeneutics* (Zondervan); *God-Centered Biblical Interpretation* (Presbyterian & Reformed); and *The Returning King: A Guide to Revelation* (Presbyterian & Reformed).

Leland Ryken is Clyde S. Kilby Professor of English at Wheaton College, where he has taught for four decades. He has published thirty books (including edited and coauthored books). Among them are *Worldly Saints* (Zondervan), *The Christian Imagination* (Baker), *The Word of God in English* (Crossway), and *Ryken's Bible Handbook* (Tyndale).

Bruce Winter is Warden and Director of the Institute for Early Christianity in the Graeco-Roman World at Tyndale House, Cambridge, Fellow of St Edmund's College, University of Cambridge, and Senior Research Fellow, Macquarie University, Sydney. He is editor of *Tyndale Bulletin,* and author of numerous articles, book chapters, and books, including *After Paul Left Corinth* (Eerdmans) and *Roman Wives, Roman Widows* (Eerdmans).

ABBREVIATIONS OF SCRIPTURE VERSIONS

CEV	Contemporary English Version
ESV	English Standard Version
GNB or TEV	Good News Bible: The Bible in Today's English Version
GW	God's Word
HCSB	Holman Christian Standard Bible
KJV	King James Version
LB	The Living Bible
MESSAGE	The Message
NASB	New American Standard Version
NCV	New Century Version
NEB	The New English Bible
NET	The NET Bible, New English Translation
NIV	New International Version
NIVI	New International Version Inclusive Language Edition
NKJV	New King James Version
NLT	New Living Translation
NRSV	New Revised Standard Version
REB	Revised English Bible
RSV	Revised Standard Version
TEV or GNB	Good News Bible: The Bible in Today's English Version
TNIV	Today's New International Version

1

ARE ONLY *SOME* WORDS OF SCRIPTURE BREATHED OUT BY GOD?

Why Plenary Inspiration Favors "Essentially Literal" Bible Translation

WAYNE GRUDEM

I. INTRODUCTION

Is Bible translation a spiritually and morally "neutral" activity, something to be guided only by secular linguistic theories about translation of languages in general? And is it true that there is really no right or wrong, no "better" or "worse" in Bible translations, but only the subjective preferences of readers who happen to "like" one translation better than another? And is the Bible such a sacred and special book that no one should ever criticize anybody else's attempts at translating the Bible?

Or might the Bible itself say something that is relevant to current debates about how the Bible should be translated?

I will argue in this chapter (1) that the Bible repeatedly claims that every one of its words (in the original languages) is a word spoken to us by God, and is therefore of utmost importance; and (2) that this fact provides a strong argument in favor of "essentially literal" (or "word-for-word") translation as opposed to "dynamic equivalent" (or "thought-for-thought") translation.

But first, some definitions:

A. Essentially Literal

An essentially literal translation translates the meaning of every word in the original language, understood correctly in its context, into its nearest English equivalent, and attempts to express the result with ordinary English word order and style, as far as that is possible without distorting the meaning of the original. Sometimes such a translation is also called a "word-for-word" translation, which is fine if we understand that at times one word in the original may be translated accurately by two or more words in English, and sometimes two or more words in the original can be represented by one word in English. The main point is that essentially literal translations attempt to represent *the meaning of every word* in the original in some way or other in the resulting translation.[1]

Sometimes essentially literal translations are called "formal equivalence" translations, suggesting that they try as far as possible to preserve the "form" of the original language in the translation. I do not generally use the phrase "formal equivalence" nor do I think it is a useful phrase for describing essentially literal translations. The reason is that the word "form" places too much emphasis on reproducing the exact word order of the original language, something that just makes for awkward translation and really has very little to do with the goal of translating the meaning of every word in the original. (The label "formal equivalence" is often used by defenders of dynamic equivalence theory, perhaps in part because this makes it so easy to caricature and thus dismiss essentially literal translation theory as a theory that places too much emphasis on the order of words in the original language.)

B. Dynamic Equivalence

A dynamic equivalence translation translates the thoughts or ideas of the original text into similar thoughts or ideas in English, and "attempts to have the same impact on modern readers as the original had on its own audience."[2] Another term for a dynamic equivalence translation is a "thought-for-thought" translation, as explained in the "Introduction"

---

[1] *The American Heritage Dictionary* (Boston and New York: Houghton Mifflin, 1996), defines "literal" as follows: "1. being in accordance with, conforming to, or upholding the exact or primary meaning of a word or words. 2. word for word; verbatim; *a literal translation* (1050).

[2] "Introduction," *Holy Bible: New Living Translation* (Wheaton, Ill.: Tyndale, 1996), xli.

to the New Living Translation (NLT): the translators say that "a dynamic-equivalence translation can also be called a thought-for-thought translation, as contrasted with a formal-equivalence or word-for-word translation."[3]

A good illustration of the difference between essentially literal and dynamic equivalence translations is actually given in the "Introduction" to the NLT. They mention 1 Kings 2:10, which says, in the King James Version, "So David slept with his fathers, and was buried in the city of David."[4] Then they note that the NLT translates this verse, "Then David died and was buried in the city of David."[5] The NLT translators see this as an advantage, for they say, "Only the New Living Translation clearly translates the real meaning of the Hebrew idiom 'slept with his fathers' into contemporary English."[6] The argument in favor of the NLT would be that today, when John Doe dies, English speakers don't say that John Doe "slept with his fathers." Today, the way we would express the idea that someone died is simply to say that John Doe "died," so that is what the NLT has done. The translation is a "thought-for-thought" translation because the main thought or idea—the idea that David died and was buried—*is expressed in a way that modern speakers would use to express the same idea today.*

However, that is not the end of the argument. Defenders of essentially literal translations object that some details are missing in the NLT's thought-for-thought translation of 1 Kings 2:10. The dynamic equivalence translation does not include the idea of sleeping as a rich metaphor for death, a metaphor in which there is a veiled hint of someday awakening from that sleep to a new life. The expression "slept with his fathers" also includes a faint hint of a corporate relationship with David's ancestors who had previously died, something that is also missing from the dynamic equivalence translation, "then David died." Critics of the NLT would agree that the NLT translated the *main idea* into contemporary English, but they would add that it is better to translate *all of the words* of the Hebrew original, including the word *shakab*

---

[3] Ibid.
[4] This same wording is followed by the NKJV, NASB, RSV, and ESV, all of which are essentially literal translations.
[5] In this chapter, underlining highlights places where I am comparing the wording of various Bible translations.
[6] "Introduction," xlii.

(which means, "to lie down, sleep"), and the words *'im* (which means "with"), and *'ab* (which means "father," and in the plural, "fathers"), since these words are in the Hebrew text as well. When these words are translated, not just the main idea but also *more details of the meaning* of the Hebrew original are brought over into English.

But will modern readers understand the literal translation, "David slept with his fathers"? Defenders of dynamic equivalence translations will say it is too difficult for readers to understand this since it is not an expression that English speakers use today. But defenders of essentially literal translations will reply that even modern readers who have never heard this idiom before will understand it because the rest of the sentence says that David was buried: "Then David slept with his fathers and was buried in the city of David" (1 Kings 2:10, ESV). The larger context begins in verse 1, "When David's time to die drew near . . ." (1 Kings 2:1). Modern readers may ponder the expression for a moment, but they will understand it, and they will then have access to the much greater richness of meaning that was there in the original text.

C. Translations Fall Along a Spectrum

Everyone involved in recent debates over Bible translations agrees that all Bible translations fall along a spectrum from those that are very literal to those that are very free or paraphrastic. This spectrum is represented on the following chart. (As the chart suggests, dynamic equivalence translations fall along a broader spectrum than essentially literal translations, because there is a wide variety in how much they are willing to paraphrase and to simplify to an easily understood idea in each verse or sentence.)

A SPECTRUM OF TRANSLATIONS

KJV	NRSV	NIV	GNB	NCV	CEV	LB	MESSAGE
NKJV	HCSB	NIVI	REB	GW			
RSV	NET	TNIV		NLT			
NASB							
ESV							

ESSENTIALLY LITERAL	MIXED	DYNAMIC EQUIVALENCE	VERY PARAPHRASTIC

Abbreviations for Bible Versions (in order of publication; dates are given for the first publication of the entire Bible in each version; second dates indicate significant revisions):

KJV	King James Version (1611)
RSV	Revised Standard Version (1952, 1971)
NASB	New American Standard Version (New American Standard Bible) (1963, 1995)
LB	The Living Bible (1971)
GNB	Good News Bible: The Bible in Today's English Version (1976, 1992)
NKJV	New King James Version (1982)
NIV	New International Version (1984)
NCV	New Century Version (1987, 1991)
REB	Revised English Bible (1989)
NRSV	New Revised Standard Version (1989)
CEV	Contemporary English Version (1995)
GW	God's Word (1995)
MESSAGE	The Message (1995)
NIVI	New International Version Inclusive Language Edition (published in UK; 1995, 1996)
NLT	New Living Translation (1996)
NET	The NET Bible, New English Translation (1996)
ESV	English Standard Version (2001)
HCSB	Holman Christian Standard Bible (2004)
TNIV	Today's New International Version (2005)

This means that in actual practice every dynamic equivalence translation still has a lot of "word-for-word" renderings of individual words in the biblical text. And every essentially literal translation has some amount of "paraphrase" where a woodenly literal translation would be nearly incomprehensible to modern readers and would hinder communication rather than helping it. One common example is Philemon 7, which in the King James Version said:

> For we have great joy and compassion in thy love, because the bowels of the saints are refreshed by thee, brother (Philem. 7, KJV).

The Greek word translated "bowels" is *splagchna,* which refers to the inward parts of the body, especially the stomach and intestines, but when not used to refer literally to those parts of the body the Greek word referred metaphorically to the seat of inward emotions or to the emotions themselves, especially love, sympathy and mercy.[7]

So how should this word be translated today? The word "bowels" is not appropriate because it has come to be used in modern English almost exclusively to refer to the intestines and the discharge of bodily waste, a sense readers in 1611 would not have given it in a verse like this. Even translating it as "the <u>intestines</u> of the saints have been refreshed by you," or "the <u>internal organs</u> of the saints have been refreshed by you," would not help modern readers, because these highly literal renderings would seem more physiological or medicinal than emotional. For that reason nearly all modern translations (including some current printings of the KJV itself) have changed to "the <u>hearts</u> of the saints have been refreshed by you" (ESV). This still talks about an internal organ (the heart) but does so in terms of an image that modern readers easily understand.[8]

But if all translations depart from complete literalness at some points, is there any difference between dynamic equivalence and essentially literal translations? Yes, there is. First, essentially literal translations will depart from complete literalness only where it is necessary, in cases where a truly literal translation would make it nearly impossible for readers to understand the meaning or would hinder communication of meaning much more than it would help it. But dynamic equivalence translations depart from literal translation and resort to paraphrase far more often, whenever the translators feel that the main thought or idea can be communicated more clearly with a more modern expression.

This reluctance to depart from literalness except where clearly necessary is reflected in the brief motto used by the translators of the 1952/1971 Revised Standard Version: "As literal as possible, as free as necessary." That motto has been subsequently used by others produc-

---

[7] W. Bauer, F. W. Danker, W. F. Arndt, and F. W. Gingrich, *A Greek-English Lexicon of the New Testament and Other Early Christian Literature* (Chicago: University of Chicago Press, 2000), 938.

[8] The term "heart" is actually within the literal range of meanings for the Greek word, since it sometimes referred to all the internal organs including the heart, lungs, liver, and kidneys (Liddell, H. G., R. Scott, and H. S. Jones, *A Greek-English Lexicon,* 9th ed. [Oxford: Clarendon, 1996], 1628).

ing essentially literal translations. The goal is *to be as literal as they can be* while still communicating the meaning clearly, and to vary from a literal to a more free translation (such as changing from "intestines" to "hearts") only where it is necessary for accurate communication.

Second, another difference is that essentially literal translations will place a high emphasis on translating *every word* of the original, as opposed to dynamic equivalence translations, which emphasize translating the thoughts more than the individual words. In the process of making an essentially literal translation, if the translators find a verse where a Greek or Hebrew word has not been translated *in some way* into English, they will count it a mistake and seek to correct it. But in dynamic equivalence translations, if the main idea has been translated correctly, the translators do not think it important to translate the meaning of every single word. (This can be demonstrated by many hundreds of examples, as will be evident below.)

In the rest of this chapter, I will argue that the things the Bible claims about its own characteristics lead to the conclusion that essentially literal translations are more compatible with the Bible's teaching about itself.

II. THE ARGUMENT FROM THE BIBLE'S TEACHING ABOUT ITS OWN WORDS

Various passages of Scripture indicate that *all* of the Bible (in the original manuscripts) is to be considered the Word of God and in fact the very words of God. Paul writes,

> *All Scripture* is breathed out by God and profitable for teaching, for reproof, for correction, and for training in righteousness (2 Tim. 3:16, ESV).

The expression "breathed out by God" is a metaphor that implies that we should think of the words of Scripture as words actually spoken by God, words that come out of his mouth and are "breathed out" by him as he speaks. This is a characteristic of "all Scripture," that is, all that Paul and the apostles would have thought to fall in the special category called "Scripture," or those writings which were of absolute divine authority for believers in the first-century church.[9] In other words, every part of Scripture is to be thought of as the words of God.

Peter writes,

> ... knowing this first of all, that no prophecy of Scripture comes from someone's own interpretation. For no prophecy was ever produced by the will of man, but men spoke from God as they were *carried along by the Holy Spirit* (2 Pet. 1:20-21, ESV).

Here Peter also emphasizes the divine origin of all the writings of Scripture, because in the immediately preceding verse, Peter referred to the whole of the Old Testament as "the prophetic word" (v. 19, ESV). Once again, Peter is emphasizing the divine nature of everything that would be considered part of the "prophetic word" or part of "Scripture." The authors of Scripture, as they wrote, were "carried along by the Holy Spirit," indicating an overall superintendence and direction of their activity such that all of Scripture is from God.

But does "all Scripture" mean the individual words themselves, or only the thoughts or ideas expressed by those words? Several texts of Scripture actually place emphasis on the individual words themselves.

For example, we read,

> *Every word* of God proves true; he is a shield to those who take refuge in him (Prov. 30:5, ESV).

Here the Hebrew expression *kol-'imrat* uses the Hebrew word *'imrah* to emphasize the actual spoken or written words of God. Every one of them is true, in the sense that the meaning that each word contributes to its overall context is reliable and trustworthy, and conforms to reality, and communicates exactly what an omniscient and all-wise God intends it to communicate.

Similarly we read in Psalm 12:

> The words of the LORD are pure words, like silver refined in a furnace on the ground, purified seven times (Ps. 12:6, ESV).

---

[9] For a discussion of the growth and extent of the canon of Scripture, see Wayne Grudem, *Systematic Theology* (Leicester, UK: InterVarsity; Grand Rapids, Mich.: Zondervan, 1994), chapter 3.

Once again, the same Hebrew word *'imrah* is used to indicate the actual spoken or written words of the Lord. They are said to be pure, so pure that they can be compared to silver that has been refined seven times. The number seven in Scripture is often used to indicate perfection. The very words of God in Scripture, then, are immeasurably pure, without any impurities in them.

Jesus expressed a similar idea when he said,

> "It is written, 'Man shall not live by bread alone, but by *every word* that comes from the mouth of God'" (Matt. 4:4, ESV).

Here the Greek term that is translated "word" is *rhēma*, which is the term Jesus would use to refer to the actual words spoken by God.[10] And the expression *"every* word" coupled with the fact that the words proceed from the "mouth of God" places further emphasis on the very words themselves. Because Jesus is repeatedly quoting from the words of Scripture in Deuteronomy in this encounter with Satan in the wilderness, the clear reference of *"every word* that comes from the mouth of God" is to the words of Scripture. Jesus' statement reminds us that we are to think of every word of Scripture as a word that comes from the mouth of God.

Finally, at the end of Revelation 22 we find a related statement:

> I warn everyone who hears the *words* of the prophecy of this book: if anyone adds to them, God will add to him the plagues described in this book, and if anyone takes away from the *words* of the book of this prophecy, God will take away his share in the tree of life and in the holy city, which are described in this book (Rev. 22:18-19, ESV).

Since John is just coming to the end of writing a book, and since he twice refers to the words of that book in this statement, the reference once again is to the individual words that are written in the book of Revelation. This is one further example of a set of passages in Scripture that emphasize the importance and divine authorship of every single word of Scripture as originally written.

---

[10] This is the same word that was used in the Septuagint translation of Deuteronomy 8:3, from which Jesus was quoting.

Sometimes Jesus and the New Testament authors make arguments from the Old Testament that depend on a single word of Scripture, a process that is consistent with this emphasis on the divine origin and authority of every word of Scripture. For example, notice Jesus' use of the Old Testament in the following dialogue between himself and some Jewish leaders:

> Now while the Pharisees were gathered together, Jesus asked them a question, saying, "What do you think about the Christ? Whose son is he?" They said to him, "The son of David." He said to them, "How is it then that David, in the Spirit, calls him Lord, saying, 'The Lord said to my Lord, Sit at my right hand, until I put your enemies under your feet'"? If then David calls him Lord, how is he his son?" (Matt. 22:41-45).

What the Jewish leaders did not understand, but what Jesus understood fully from the knowledge of his own deity and humanity, is that in the expression, "The Lord said to my Lord," the expression "the Lord" is a reference to God the Father while the expression "my Lord" is a reference to Christ himself, who is both descended from David and the eternal second person of the Trinity whom David can call his "Lord."

In order for Jesus' argument to work, he has to depend on the accuracy of the word "my" in the expression "my Lord," and in Hebrew that is expressed by a single letter, the letter *yod,* which is the smallest letter in the Hebrew alphabet. If the handwritten form of that letter had been a little longer it would have meant, "his Lord." If it had been a little longer still, it would have meant, "your Lord." So here Jesus depends on the accuracy of a single letter in the Hebrew text of the Old Testament and trusts it to make an argument about the identity of the Messiah. This is not surprising: he considered every word to be a word from God.

Jesus emphasized a similar confidence in every detail of the Old Testament when he said,

> "For truly, I say to you, until heaven and earth pass away, not an iota, not a dot, will pass from the Law until all is accomplished" (Matt. 5:18, ESV).

In this statement, the expression "not an iota, not a dot" refers to the smallest letter in the Hebrew alphabet (the letter *yod*) and then to a small part of a letter in the Old Testament Scriptures. All is from God; none will pass away.

In Galatians 3:16, Paul bases an argument on the difference between singular and plural forms of a word:

> Now the promises were made to Abraham and to his offspring. It does not say, "And to offsprings," referring to many, but referring to one, "And to your offspring," who is Christ.

In this argument Paul depends not on the general thought of an Old Testament passage but on the specific form of one word in the Old Testament.

Roger Nicole, in a significant essay in 1958, listed many more New Testament passages where the argument of Jesus or the New Testament author depended on a single word in the Old Testament. He gives the following list: Matthew 2:15; 4:10; 13:35; 22:44; Mark 12:36; Luke 4:8; 20:42, 43; John 8:17; 10:34; 19:37; Acts 23:5; Romans 4:3, 9, 23; 15:9-12; 1 Corinthians 6:16; Galatians 3:8, 10, 13, 16; Hebrews 1:7; 2:12; 3:13; 4:7; 12:26.[11] This is not surprising: if every word is from God, every word can be trusted completely.

III. IF ALL THE WORDS ARE FROM GOD, THEN TRANSLATORS SHOULD TRANSLATE NO LESS THAN THE ORIGINAL.

If we are convinced that all the words of Scripture in the original manuscripts are from God, then it is important to focus on accurately translating the meaning of each word in its context. Translators should not only ask, "Have I rendered the main idea of this sentence correctly?" but should also ask, "Have I represented correctly *the meaning that each word contributes to this sentence?*" This is because every word contributes something to the meaning, whether by providing additional

---

[11] Roger Nicole, "New Testament Use of the Old Testament," in *Revelation and the Bible*, ed. Carl F. H. Henry (Grand Rapids, Mich.: Baker, 1958), 139.

information, or by adding emphasis or nuance, or by modifying the meaning of the text in some other way.

(I realize that some Hebrew and Greek words may not always be translated by an English word, such as the Greek conjunction *de,* which often signifies merely a transition to the next thought and may be represented in English only by a comma, or by the beginning of a new sentence, or even by the way in which clauses are arranged in relationship to one another. But in each of those cases the word *de* still represents *some meaning,* and those are various devices by which the meaning may be brought over into English. There are other cases where a word just adds emphasis, as with a Hebrew participle combined with a cognate finite verb, and this may be conveyed in English just by the arrangement of words, or by the choice of a single strong verb, but in each case the translation still attempts to represent *in some way* the meaning that each word in the original contributed to the sentence.)

This attempt to translate the meaning of each word in the original as accurately as possible is the philosophy behind essentially literal translations. This would include, in earlier periods, the King James Version (or Authorized Version), the English Revised Version of 1881, and the American Standard Version of 1901. Among more recent translations, this is the philosophy that has been followed by the English Standard Version, the Revised Standard Version, the New Revised Standard Version (except for gender language), the New King James Version, the New American Standard Bible, the NET Bible, and the Holman Christian Standard Bible.

IV. DYNAMIC EQUIVALENCE TRANSLATIONS OFTEN LEAVE OUT THE MEANINGS OF SOME WORDS THAT ARE IN THE ORIGINAL TEXT.

In contrast to essentially literal translations, dynamic equivalence translations, by virtue of their translation theory, often fail to translate the meaning that some of the words contribute to the verse or sentence in the original. Some examples of this tendency can be seen in the material that follows.

1. *The Missing Sword*

In discussing the role of civil government, Paul says that the civil authority has the right to "bear the sword" in his role as a "servant of God":

> . . . he is God's servant for your good. But if you do wrong, be afraid, for he does not <u>bear the sword</u> in vain. For he is the servant of God, an avenger who carries out God's wrath on the wrongdoer (Rom. 13:4, ESV).

The Greek word translated "sword" is *machaira,* which simply means "sword." All essentially literal translations use the word "sword" to translate this word: KJV, NKJV, RSV, NRSV, NASB, NET, ESV, and HCSB. In addition, the NIV, which lies between essentially literal and dynamic equivalence translation, also uses the word "sword."

But some dynamic equivalence translations omit the word "sword." The New Living Translation says:

> The authorities are sent by God to help you. But if you are doing something wrong, of course you should be afraid, <u>for you will be punished</u>. The authorities are established by God for that very purpose, to punish those who do wrong.

The NLT has changed a statement about the civil authority ("<u>he</u> does not bear the sword in vain") to a statement about the reader ("<u>you</u> will be punished"). There is no mention of the sword.

The New Century Version does something similar:

> The ruler is God's servant to help you. But if you do wrong, then be afraid. <u>He has the power to punish</u>; he is God's servant to punish those who do wrong.

Once again there is no mention of a sword. But was the word *machaira* breathed out by God like the other words in Scripture? Then why not translate it?

The Contemporary English Version similarly omits the sword:

If you do something wrong, you ought to be afraid because these rulers <u>have the right to punish you</u>.

The Message strays even further from the sense of the text:

But if you're breaking the rules right and left, watch out. The police <u>aren't there just to be admired in their uniforms</u>.

Perhaps supporters of dynamic equivalence translations would respond that "he has the power to punish" is stating *the same idea* as "he does not bear the sword in vain," but doing it in a contemporary way of speaking about government authority. *But is it the same idea?* This is one of the primary verses appealed to by Christian ethicists who defend the right of the civil government in the New Testament era to carry out capital punishment. The right to "bear the sword" involves the authority to do exactly what the sword was used for—to put someone to death. This same word *machaira* is used in Acts 12:2 to say that Herod "killed James the brother of John with the *sword.*" It is also used to speak about persecution, in Hebrews 11:37: "they were killed with the *sword.*" The argument is this: if the state has the power to "bear the sword," it has the power to carry out capital punishment.

Those who oppose capital punishment argue that Paul mentions the "sword" here only as a symbol of governmental authority and this does not imply the power to take life.[12] People may or may not find this a persuasive explanation of the "sword" in Romans 13:4, but readers of the NLT, NCV, CEV, and The Message cannot even follow the argument. They could never even *think* of such an argument from this verse, because there is no mention of bearing the sword. "Punishment" might mean only jail time. Or community service. Or a fine. When I teach ethics, I could never use these dynamic equivalence translations to argue for capital punishment from this verse because they have not translated all the words.

All the words of Scripture are breathed out by God for purposes

---

[12] For the pro-capital punishment position regarding the power of the sword, see John Feinberg and Paul Feinberg, *Ethics for a Brave New World* (Wheaton, Ill.: Crossway, 1993), 139, 145; and for the anti-capital punishment argument on the power of the sword, see Glen Stassen and David Gushee, *Kingdom Ethics* (Downers Grove, Ill.: InterVarsity, 2003), 207.

only he fully understood. He put the words there so that we could use them to probe deeper into the meaning of Scripture and even to construct arguments or to answer arguments yet to be invented in the future. But some of these words of God are simply deleted from dynamic equivalence translations. Unless our theory of translation seeks to translate all the *words* (in some way or another), we will leave out things that we don't know we are leaving out, and we will leave out part of the meaning of Scripture.

Are only *some* words of Scripture breathed out by God?

2. *Removing the Wrath of God*

In this same passage (Romans 13) another important element is Paul's affirmation of the fact that the civil government is God's servant who carries out the wrath of God on criminal offenders:

> For he is God's servant for your good. But if you do wrong, be afraid, for he does not bear the sword in vain. For he is the servant of God, an avenger who carries out <u>God's wrath</u> on the wrongdoer (Rom. 13:4, ESV).

The word translated "wrath" is *orgē*, which means "wrath" and is translated with the word "wrath" by almost all essentially literal translations: it is the reading of the KJV, NKJV, RSV, NRSV, NASB, ESV, and HCSB.

But a number of dynamic equivalence translations leave out the wrath of God and simply mention punishment:

> The authorities are established by God for that very purpose <u>to punish those who do wrong</u> (NLT).

> He is God's servant <u>to punish those who do wrong</u> (NCV).

> The police aren't there just to be admired in their uniforms. <u>God also has an interest in keeping order, and he uses them to do it</u> (MESSAGE).

Why is it important to mention God's wrath in this verse? First, because it ties directly back to Romans 12:19:

Beloved, never avenge yourselves, but leave it to the <u>wrath of God</u>, for it is written, "Vengeance is mine, I will repay, says the Lord" (ESV).

Paul tells people not to take personal revenge but to leave it to God's wrath: he will avenge wrongdoing. Then just a few verses later in Romans 13:4 he explains one situation in which this happens: God's wrath is expressed through the penalties imposed by the civil government. When the government punishes a criminal, Paul says that the punishment is actually carrying out the wrath of God against the criminal. When this is coupled with Romans 12:19, it provides a strong incentive for people not to seek personal vengeance but to allow the God-appointed civil government to punish the criminal. However, this argument cannot be made from these dynamic equivalence translations. They included one main idea (punishment) but left out a crucial detail (God's wrath).

The second reason it is important to mention the wrath of God is that it shows that government has a retributive function in administering criminal punishments. The phrase "to punish" in dynamic equivalence translations is too weak because punishment may simply be for the purpose of deterring future crime or educating people through discipline. Punishment need not have any connection with the wrath of God or with the idea of actually bringing retribution on the wrongdoer.

But to be "a servant of God, an avenger who carries out <u>God's wrath</u> on the wrongdoer" implies retribution: the one who did wrong is to be justly paid back. The punishment is not just to train the criminal, and it is not just to prevent more crime, but it is also to bring retribution to satisfy the demands of God's justice, at least partially in this present age. In this way the verse provides profound insight into the ultimate justification for retributive punishment carried out by the civil government: such punishment manifests the just wrath of God.

But the wrath of God is missing from the NLT, the NCV, and the Message at this point. Why? Is not the Greek word *orgē* a word that was breathed out by God? Are only some words of Scripture breathed out by God? Should we not translate *all* the words of God?

3. The Missing Hands

Several passages of the New Testament refer to the common practice of Jesus and his disciples to place their hands on people when they healed them. Apparently the crowds understood this to be such a common practice for Jesus that one of the rulers of the synagogue asked Jesus at one point, "My little daughter is at the point of death. Come and <u>lay your hands on her</u> so that she may be made well and live" (Mark 5:23, ESV). He just assumed that that was how Jesus healed. When the New Testament tells specific stories about the healing of specific individual persons, both essentially literal and dynamic equivalence translations report this accurately— they tell us that Jesus laid his hands on someone and the person was healed.

But when the New Testament reports *summary statements* that refer to this frequent practice of Jesus or the disciples laying hands on people, all essentially literal translations faithfully translate the word "hands" but dynamic equivalence translations tend simply to leave the word out, as is evident in the following verses:

Mark 6:2:

> . . . and many who heard him were astonished, saying, "Where did this man get these things? What is the wisdom given to him? How are such mighty works done <u>by his hands</u>?" (ESV; the word "hands" is the plural form of the Greek word *cheir*, which means "hand"; the word "hands" is found in all essentially literal translations: see KJV, NKJV, RSV, NRSV, NASB, NET, ESV, and HCSB).

> . . . and many who heard him were amazed. "Where did this man get these things?" they asked. "What's this wisdom that has been given him, that <u>he</u> even does miracles!" (NIV; the word "hands" is similarly omitted from TNIV, NLT, CEV, NCV, MESSAGE).

Acts 5:12:

> Now many signs and wonders were regularly done among the people <u>by the hands</u> of the apostles (ESV; "hands" is used to translate Greek *cheir* also in KJV, NKJV, RSV, NASB, NET, ESV, HCSB).

The apostles performed many miraculous signs and wonders among the people (NIV; the word "hands" is similarly omitted from TNIV, NLT, CEV, NCV, MESSAGE).

Acts 14:3:

So they remained for a long time, speaking boldly for the Lord, who bore witness to the word of his grace, granting signs and wonders to be done by their hands (ESV; "hands" is also found in KJV, NKJV, RSV, NASB, NET; the HCSB uncharacteristically leaves it out at this verse).

So Paul and Barnabas spent considerable time there, speaking boldly for the Lord, who confirmed the message of his grace by enabling *them* to do miraculous signs and wonders. (NIV; the word "hands" is similarly omitted from TNIV, NLT, CEV, NCV, MESSAGE).

Acts 19:11:

And God was doing extraordinary miracles by the hands of Paul (ESV; "hands" in KJV, NKJV, RSV, NASB, NET, HCSB).

God did extraordinary miracles through Paul (NIV; the word "hands" is similarly omitted from TNIV, NLT, CEV, NCV, MESSAGE).

So the word "hands" is missing from most dynamic equivalence translations in these key summary verses, and it is also missing from the NIV and TNIV, reflecting their tendency to use dynamic equivalence translations more often than essentially literal translations.[13]

Why is this important? When I teach classes on spiritual gifts I often point to a common pattern of Jesus and the apostles in which they laid

---

[13] The plural "hands" in these verses makes these expressions unlike the singular "hand" in the Old Testament Hebrew idiom "by the hand of" (*beyad*, singular, as in Josh. 14:2 and over thirty times in the Old Testament), indicating the agent by which something is done. Therefore these expressions should not be seen as a mere idiom rather than a literal description of what happened. Moreover, there is an evident connection between these summary statements about miracles done through Jesus' or the apostles' hands and the numerous specific narratives where they laid their hands on an individual person for healing, and this would lead readers to readily give "hands" a literal meaning in these verses.

their hands on sick people as they ministered to them. The verses above that give a general summary of their ministries show that the pattern was more common than we might deduce from seeing a few specific examples in the gospels. I can make that point from almost any essentially literal translation, but the point is entirely missing from dynamic equivalence translations and even from the NIV and TNIV, which have some dynamic equivalence tendencies. Defenders of these translations might say that they used a "thought-for-thought" philosophy and told us the main idea—that God was working miracles through Jesus and Paul and the other apostles. I would agree that they gave us something similar to the idea in these verses, but they didn't get the details right. They failed several times to translate the word "hands." But is this not a word that was breathed out by God? Is this not part of God's Word to us? Are only some of the words of Scripture breathed out by God?

4. *The Lost Soul*

Just before his crucifixion, Jesus expressed his deep anguish:

> "Now is my <u>soul</u> troubled. And what shall I say? 'Father, save me from this hour'? But for this purpose I have come to this hour" (John 12:27, ESV).

The word translated "soul" is *psychē,* a term that can mean either "soul" or "life," depending on the context. Essentially literal translations all translate it as "soul" here (KJV, NKJV, RSV, NRSV, NASB, NET, ESV, HCSB). But dynamic equivalence translations mostly omit the word "soul" completely, substituting some other word instead:[14]

> "Now my <u>heart</u> is troubled" (NIV).

> "Now <u>I</u> am very troubled" (NCV).

> "Now <u>I</u> am deeply troubled" (CEV).

> "Right now <u>I</u> am storm-tossed" (MESSAGE).

---

[14] TNIV and NLT correctly have "soul" here.

This verse is important for countering the ancient heresy of Apollinarianism, the idea that Jesus only had a human body, not a human soul or spirit. If Jesus' "soul" was troubled, then he had a human soul as well as body and was able to experience emotions similar to what we experience. I use this verse in teaching theology students about the person of Christ (lest they fall into Apollinarianism themselves). I also use this verse in teaching about the nature of our souls. But I cannot teach these things from dynamic equivalence translations of this verse. Jesus' soul is missing from the verse in those translations.

5. The Lost Spirit

A verse related to John 12:27 occurs in the next chapter of John:

> After saying these things, Jesus was troubled in his spirit, and testified, "Truly, truly, I say to you, one of you will betray me" (John 13:21, ESV).

The word translated "spirit" is *pneuma,* which here means "spirit." This word is translated "spirit" by all essentially literal translations, including the KJV, NKJV, RSV, NRSV, NASB, NET, ESV, and HCSB, as well as by the NIV, TNIV, and NLT. But some dynamic equivalence translations omit "spirit":

> After Jesus said this, he was very troubled (NCV).

> After Jesus had said these things, he was deeply troubled . . . (CEV).

> After he said these things, Jesus became visibly upset . . . (MESSAGE).

Did they get the general idea right? Yes, approximately. Did they preserve all the important details? No, for that is not the goal of a "thought-for-thought" or dynamic equivalence translation.

This verse is also important when I teach theology, for several reasons: (1) it shows that Jesus had a human spirit that could be troubled, providing another argument against the Apollinarian heresy; (2) the parallel with a similar statement in John 12:27 is one indication that "soul" and "spirit" may be two different terms for the same thing; (3) the fact that Jesus could perceive things in his spirit encourages us also to pay attention to what is happening in our own human spirits in various circumstances. But none of this can be argued from the NCV, the CEV, or The Message because Jesus' spirit is missing from the verse in those translations.

A similar loss of a person's human spirit is found in Luke's gospel, in the story of Mary coming to visit Elizabeth:

> And Mary said, "My <u>soul</u> magnifies the Lord, and my <u>spirit</u> rejoices in God my Savior . . ." (Luke 1:46-47, ESV).

The verse contains both the Greek word for "soul" (*psychē*) and the Greek word for "spirit" (*pneuma*). Essentially literal translations all translate them as "soul" and "spirit" (KJV, NKJV, RSV, NRSV, NASB, NET, ESV, and HCSB; in addition, the NIV and TNIV also have "soul" and "spirit" here).

But dynamic equivalence translations leave out Mary's spirit and mostly leave out her soul as well:

> Mary responded, "Oh, how <u>I</u> praise the Lord. How <u>I</u> rejoice in God my Savior!" (NLT).

> Then Mary said, "My soul praises the Lord; my <u>heart</u> rejoices in God my Savior" (NCV).

> Mary said: "With all my <u>heart</u> I praise the Lord, and <u>I</u> am glad because of God my Savior" (CEV).

> And Mary said, "<u>I'm</u> bursting with God-news; <u>I'm</u> dancing the song of my Savior God" (MESSAGE).

When this verse is translated literally and "soul" and "spirit" are included, the doctrinal implications of the verse are significant: (1) Since the two halves of Mary's statement follow the pattern of Hebrew poetic parallelism (repeating the same idea with slightly different words or nuances), this verse also provides evidence that "soul" and "spirit" may be used as different words for the same thing; and (2) since Mary was aware of the fact that her spirit was rejoicing, this gives warrant for thinking that we too can be aware of what our spirits are doing or feeling. But these ideas could not be taught from the NLT, CEV, NCV, or The Message, because those versions omit Mary's human spirit from the passage.

6. *The Disappearing Rod of Discipline*

The book of Proverbs is quite explicit about the need for physical discipline of children:

> Whoever spares the <u>rod</u> hates his son, but he who loves him is diligent to discipline him (Prov. 13:24, ESV).

The word translated "rod" is *shēbet,* meaning "rod, staff." It is translated as "rod" in all essentially literal translations: KJV, NKJV, RSV, NRSV, NASB, NET, ESV, and HCSB.

But the "rod," giving justification for spanking or similar use of a physical object for discipline, is omitted from several dynamic equivalence translations:

> If you refuse to <u>discipline</u> your children, it proves you don't love them; if you love your children, you will be prompt to discipline them (NLT).

> If you do not <u>punish</u> your children, you don't love them, but if you love your children, you will correct them (NCV).

> If you love your children, you will <u>correct</u> them; if you don't love them, you won't correct them (CEV).

> A refusal to <u>correct</u> is a refusal to love; love your children by disciplining them (MESSAGE).

The same omission of the "rod" (Hebrew *shēbet*) is found in Proverbs 22:15. All essentially literal translations use "rod" in this verse, as in the ESV:

> Folly is bound up in the heart of a child, but the <u>rod</u> of discipline drives it far from him (ESV; similarly, KJV, NKJV, RSV, NRSV, NASB, NET, ESV, HCSB).

But "rod" it is omitted from dynamic equivalence translations:

A youngster's heart is filled with foolishness, but <u>discipline</u> will drive it away (NLT).

Every child is full of foolishness, but <u>punishment</u> can get rid of it (NCV).

All children are foolish, but <u>firm correction</u> will make them change (CEV).

Young people are prone to foolishness and fads; the cure comes through <u>tough-minded discipline</u> (MESSAGE).

Political activists who campaign for laws prohibiting all spanking of children may face no objections from Christians who read the dynamic equivalence translations of these verses. The rod of discipline is removed, and the verses just talk about discipline and punishment, which can take many non-physical forms. The "thought-for-thought" translators got the general idea approximately right (discipline of children) but they just happened to leave out the meaning of a specific word that is unpopular in today's culture. Is the word *shēbet* ("rod") not breathed out by God? Is it not a word God wants his people to have?

7. *The Lost Faces*

Paul speaks about some future time in this way:

> For now we see in a mirror dimly, but then <u>face to face</u>. Now I know in part; then I shall know fully, even as I have been fully known (1 Cor. 13:12, ESV).

The Greek phrase *prosōpon pros prosōpon* is translated literally as "face to face" in all essentially literal translations: KJV, NKJV, RSV, NRSV, NASB, NET, ESV, and HCSB. It is important because it echoes an Old Testament background where seeing "face to face" is mentioned six times and every time it refers to seeing God.[15] So Paul is saying that "then," at that future time, we will see God face to face—and that must

---

[15] See Grudem, *Systematic Theology*, 1033n.24; or the more detailed discussion in Wayne Grudem, *The Gift of Prophecy in the New Testament and Today* (Wheaton, Ill.: Crossway, 2000), 196-197.

be the time when Christ returns. When Christ returns, then we will see God *face to face* (see Rev. 22:4).

This verse has been important in discussions about spiritual gifts, especially gifts like prophecy and speaking in tongues. Should we expect that they will continue today? Just four verses earlier Paul says, "As for prophecies, they will pass away; as for tongues, they will cease; as for knowledge, it will pass away" (1 Cor. 13:8, ESV). When will this happen? If it is connected with the "then" when we see God "face to face" in verse 12 (as some people have argued, including me), then we can expect prophecies and tongues to continue until the time Christ returns. Other scholars have argued against this interpretation,[16] but whatever view someone takes, the phrase "face to face" is important to the whole argument.

However, readers of several dynamic equivalence translations cannot even understand the discussion. The literal translation "face to face" has been eliminated:

> Now we see things imperfectly as in a poor mirror, but then we will see everything with perfect clarity. All that I know now is partial and incomplete, but then I will know everything completely, just as God knows me now (1 Cor. 13:12, NLT).

> It is the same with us. Now we see a dim reflection as if we were looking into a mirror, but then we shall see clearly (NCV).

> But it won't be long before the weather clears and the sun shines bright! (MESSAGE).

Editors of these translations probably thought they were representing the main thought of this clause: something to do with seeing clearly. But by failing to translate word for word they missed the whole connection with the Old Testament background of seeing God "face to face." Were the words *prosōpon pros prosōpon* not breathed out by God? Why should translations omit some of God's words?

---

[16] See the extensive discussion in Wayne Grudem, editor, *Are Miraculous Gifts for Today? Four Views* (Grand Rapids, Mich.: Zondervan, 1996), especially the discussions by Richard Gaffin, page 55, and Robert Saucy, pages 123-124, and other literature that they cite.

8. *The Lost Kiss*

In several passages Paul encourages Christians to greet one another with a "holy kiss," as he does at the end of Romans:

> Greet one another with a <u>holy kiss</u> (Rom. 16:16, ESV).

The Greek word *philēma* means "kiss" and the word *hagios* is the very common word meaning "holy." All essentially literal translations render this expression "holy kiss" (so KJV, NKJV, RSV, NRSV, NASB, NET, ESV, and HCSB).

This expression is important today in part because Christians are sometimes puzzled over how to explain why we don't follow this command today. We feel bound to obey most of the commands written to Christians in the New Testament epistles—so why not this one? On the other hand, if we can obey this command in a different way today, such as through a warm greeting or handshake, then should we feel free to change the way we obey other New Testament commands? Just how many commands are "culturally relative," and how can we tell which ones are? As it turns out, thinking through this problem provides us with valuable understanding about the nature of the New Testament and how its commands apply to us today.

I have written about this question elsewhere, and will not go into detail about it here.[17] But in order to understand the discussion, and to know why it presents somewhat of a challenge, readers have to know that Paul speaks of a "holy kiss."

However, readers of some dynamic equivalence translations will not even know there is a problem of application here, for the "holy kiss" is missing.

> Greet each other in <u>Christian love</u>. (NLT).

> Be sure to give each other a <u>warm greeting</u> (CEV).

> <u>Holy embraces</u> all around! (MESSAGE).

---

[17] See Wayne Grudem, *Evangelical Feminism and Biblical Truth* (Sisters, Ore.: Multnomah, 2004), 397-402.

Paul could easily have written the Greek equivalent for "Christian love" or "warm greeting" or "holy embraces" if he had wanted to. But those things are not what he wrote. He wrote, "Greet one another with a holy kiss." Even if we agree that we should use another kind of greeting today, should we not first *translate* the words accurately *so that readers can know exactly what Paul was saying at that time?* Translating the Bible is not the same as preaching a sermon or writing an ethics textbook or telling people what they should do today. Bible translators should just translate accurately, not give us their ideas of contemporary application. The words of the Bible are God's words, and we should translate them as carefully as possible, not change them to say something different. Are the words "with a holy kiss" (Greek *en philēmati hagiō*) not breathed out by God?

9. The Missing Heart and the Absent Holy Spirit

Generations of Christians have identified with David's famous words of repentance in Psalm 51:

> Create in me a <u>clean heart</u>, O God,
> and renew a right spirit within me.
> <u>Cast me not away from your presence</u>,
> and <u>take not your Holy Spirit from me</u> (Ps. 51:10-11, ESV).

All essentially literal translations include the same elements of this prayer: a request for a "clean heart" (or a "pure heart") and right spirit from God, and a plea that God not cast the person from his presence or remove his Holy Spirit.

But look at The Message on this passage:

> God, make a <u>fresh start</u> in me,
> shape a Genesis week from the chaos of my life.
> <u>Don't throw me out with the trash</u>,
> or <u>fail to breathe holiness in me</u>.

On first reading The Message on this passage people might think, "How creative!" "How catchy!" "What an interesting way to put it!" But then we realize: *creating new ideas* is not what translators are to do.

We have no business creating things God did not say. Why should anyone think it right to invent new metaphors that God did not use ("Don't throw me out with the trash") and omit clear wording that he did use ("Cast me not away from your presence")? This kind of material belongs in sermons; it does not belong in a book that says "The Bible" on the cover.

V. DYNAMIC EQUIVALENCE TRANSLATIONS OFTEN ADD MEANING THAT IS NOT IN THE ORIGINAL TEXT.

When dynamic equivalence translations attempt only to render the main idea of a phrase or verse, *they often add components of meaning* that are not in the original text. As a result, English Bible readers will think something is in Scripture that is not.

1. *Restrictions to What God Provides*

Paul writes to Timothy about those who are rich in this world:

> As for the rich in this present age, charge them not to be haughty, nor to set their hopes on the uncertainty of riches, but on God, who richly provides us with <u>everything</u> to enjoy (1 Tim. 6:17, ESV).

The Greek word translated "everything" is *panta,* the accusative form of the word *pas,* a common word meaning "everything." All essentially literal translations render this literally as "everything" or "all things" with nothing else added to it (KJV, NKJV, RSV, NRSV, NASB, NET, ESV, HCSB). This verse tells me I can freely enjoy the abundant diversity of God's excellent creation, giving thanks to him for everything that he gives.

But the New Living Translation and the Contemporary English Version insert an entirely different idea:

> Tell those who are rich in this world not to be proud and not to trust in their money, which will soon be gone. But their trust should be in the living God, who richly gives us <u>all we need</u> for our enjoyment (NLT).

> Tell them to have faith in God, who is rich and blesses us with <u>every-thing we need</u> to enjoy life (CEV).

Paul could have said "everything we need" but he did not. He did not limit it that way. Perhaps the NLT and CEV translators were uncomfortable with the idea that God richly gives us *everything* to enjoy, so they decided to let us enjoy only the things we "need." But they have added "we need" to the Bible: there is nothing in the Greek text that means that or says that or restricts our enjoyment of God's abundant creation in that way.

2. Added Elders

In writing instructions to Timothy, Paul says:

> Do not be hasty in <u>the laying on of hands,</u> nor take part in the sins of others; keep yourself pure (1 Tim. 5:22, ESV).

Most essentially literal translations speak of laying on of hands in this verse (KJV, NKJV, RSV, NASB, NET, ESV, and HCSB).

But the New Living Translation omits laying on of hands and adds words about elders here, words Paul did not say:

> Never be in a hurry about <u>appointing an elder</u>. Do not participate in the sins of others. Keep yourself pure.

Paul talks about elders elsewhere, and there is a good Greek word for "elder" that he uses (*presbuteros*) in those verses, but he did not use it here. He did not speak of appointing "an elder," but about laying on of hands. He probably meant to include laying on of hands to establish elders in office, but what about laying on of hands to establish deacons? And what about laying on of hands to send people out on missionary journeys? Why does the NLT decide it can add "an elder" and thus limit the application to elders, when Paul did not limit it in what he wrote? When we add words to Scripture in this way, we often add restrictions to the original statements that the author did not intend or have in mind.

3. Teachers Who Can Never Get Anything Right

James warns that even teachers (including himself) make mistakes or "stumble":

> Not many of you should become teachers, my brothers, for you know that we who teach will be judged with greater strictness. [2] For <u>we all stumble in many ways</u>, and if anyone does not stumble in what he says, he is a perfect man, able also to bridle his whole body (James 3:1-2, ESV; other essentially literal translations are similar, and the Greek word *ptaio* simply means "to stumble, lose one's footing").

James does not say that he ("we all") is always wrong or even that he is often wrong (he is an apostle writing Scripture!). He does not say that teachers in the church are always wrong or often wrong (or how could anyone trust them?). He just says that everyone is still imperfect—we stumble "in many ways." There is sin of various kinds that remains in our hearts, and we do make mistakes of various kinds.

But that is far different from what James is made to say in The Message:

> And none of us is perfectly qualified. <u>We get it wrong nearly every time we open our mouths</u> (James 3:2, MESSAGE).

James never said that teachers "get it wrong nearly every time" they open their mouths! That would mean the readers should hardly believe anything an elder or a teacher says in church. That would mean that James himself "got it wrong" nearly every time he said anything. This gives a horrible picture of unreliability even for the speech of an apostle. But "nearly every time we open our mouths" is just a set of words that The Message has added to the Bible. Nothing in the Greek text gives anything close to that meaning. The whole phrase is just a "creative" addition to the words of God. But the phrase is not the words of God, and it does not belong in the Bible. Why do dynamic equivalence translators think they can add whole new ideas to the Bible?

4. Boasting About Being Wise as the Worst Kind of Lie

James warns his readers not to boast:

> But if you have bitter jealousy and selfish ambition in your hearts, do not boast and be false to the truth (James 3:14, ESV; identical translations, or similar translations such as "lie against the truth" are found in the essentially literal translations of the KJV, NKJV, RSV, NASB, NET, and HCSB).

But the New Living Translation adds an entirely different idea:

> But if you are bitterly jealous and there is selfish ambition in your hearts, don't brag about being wise. That is the worst kind of lie (NLT).

Where did "the worst kind" come from? Nothing in the Greek text says anything like this, or talks about boasting being worse than other lies. Is boasting really worse than a lie that leads to someone's death or suicide, or a lie that destroys someone's reputation or marriage? Is it really worse than a lie that betrays one's entire country? Is it worse than a lie that leads someone to reject Christ? The NLT has just added words here that are not true, and are not part of the Word of God.

VI. THE RESULT: CAN WE TRUST DYNAMIC EQUIVALENCE TRANSLATIONS?

The examples I have mentioned are only the tip of the iceberg. I put them together in a few hours, and thousands more could be found by looking anywhere and everywhere in dynamic equivalence translations. Such omissions or additions of details of meaning are pervasive in these translations because they belong to the dynamic equivalence philosophy of thought-for-thought translation. The goal of dynamic equivalence translators is to express the primary thought of each passage or verse clearly but they see no need to translate the meaning of every word, and they see nothing wrong with adding some details or expressions that they think will make the primary thought more clear or vivid.

When I look at examples like these I know I cannot teach theology or ethics classes using a dynamic equivalence translation. There are too many details of meaning missing, details that are often important for theology. And there are too many details added, details that will lead people down paths of thought that are not part of God's Word.

Although the NIV is not a thoroughly dynamic equivalence translation, there is so much dynamic equivalence influence in the NIV that I cannot teach theology or ethics from it either. I tried it for one semester several years ago, shortly after the NIV first came out, and I gave it up after a few weeks. Time and again I would try to use a verse to make a point and find that the specific detail I was looking for, a detail of wording that I knew was there in the original Hebrew or Greek, was missing from the verse in the NIV.

Nor can I preach from a dynamic equivalence translation. I would end up explaining in verse after verse that the words on the page are not really what the Bible says, and the whole experience would be confusing and would lead people not to trust the Bible in English but to distrust it.

Nor can I teach an adult Bible class at my church using a dynamic equivalence translation without checking the original language at every verse. I would never know what words to trust or what words have been left out.

Nor can I lead our home fellowship group using a dynamic equivalence translation. People have sometimes brought the New Living Translation or The Message to a Bible study and I've seen them get excited about seeing some new ideas in a verse, but I have to bite my tongue because I know that the new idea they see in the verse is not there in the Greek or Hebrew text. I don't want to discourage their excitement about contributing to the Bible study, but I just wish they would be excited about something that is actually in the Word of God.

Nor would I ever want to memorize passages from a dynamic equivalence translation. I would be fixing in my brain verses that were partly God's words and partly some added ideas, and I would be leaving out of my brain some words that belonged to those verses as God inspired them but were simply missing from the dynamic equivalence translation.

But I could readily use *any* modern essentially literal translation (especially the ESV, NASB, NET BIBLE, and HCSB)[18] to teach, study, preach from, and memorize. The wording may differ slightly, but the words are all there and the meaning is all there as completely as it can be expressed in English.

What then can I do with dynamic equivalence translations like the New Living Translation or The Message? I can read them like I read a commentary, not thinking of them as exactly the Word of God, but as a fresh and creative way to convey an *explanation* of the verse or an *interpretation* of the verse as understood by some very competent evangelical scholars. I think of these versions as skillful free *interpretations* of Scripture, but not strictly as *translations*.

VII. THE THEORY OF DYNAMIC EQUIVALENCE IS THE CULPRIT BEHIND THESE MISSING AND ADDED WORDS.

How did this situation come about? Where did we get all these dynamic equivalence translations? The primary influence behind them has been translation specialist Eugene Nida and his advocacy of dynamic equivalence translations.

Nida earned a Ph.D. in linguistics at the University of Michigan in 1943. He published *Toward a Science of Translating* (Leiden: Brill) in 1964 and *The Theory and Practice of Translation* (Leiden: Brill) in 1969. These two books, in addition to Nida's monumental personal

---

[18] Four other essentially literal translations are the KJV (1611), NKJV (1982), the RSV (1952/1971) and the NRSV (1989). They also have value but I find them less useful for various reasons:

The KJV was an amazingly good translation for its day, but the English is now nearly 400 years old and sounds increasingly archaic and foreign to modern readers.

The NKJV translation is also an excellent translation, but the New Testament is based on inferior Greek manuscripts. The NKJV committee decided to base their work on the Greek manuscripts that were used by the original KJV translators in 1611 instead of taking into account the thousands of older and more reliable Greek manuscripts that archaeologists have discovered in the nearly 400 years since that time. No point of doctrine is affected, but it does affect many details of many verses, and that manuscript decision means that the NKJV will never become the standard English version used by the vast majority of New Testament scholars and seminary-trained pastors around the world.

The RSV of 1952/1971 was a very good, essentially literal translation but was never widely accepted by evangelicals because of theologically liberal influences on some key verses, such as the removal of "virgin" from Isaiah 7:14, the removal of Messianic predictions from some Old Testament passages such as Psalm 2:12 and 45:6, the frequent editorial decision to emend the Hebrew text at many difficult Old Testament verses, and the removal of the term "propitiation" from some key New Testament verses. The RSV also has the disadvantage of retaining archaic "Thee" and "Thou" in prayers and praises to God.

The NRSV of 1989 was in many ways a helpful update of the RSV, but its decision to use gender-neutral language resulted in a distortion of the meaning of the original text and the incorrect removal of "father," "son," "brother," "man," and "he/him/his" from around 4000 verses, and this has meant that it will never gain widespread acceptance among evangelical Christians.

influence on the American Bible Society, the United Bible Societies, and the Summer Institute of Linguistics (SIL), have influenced thousands of Bible translators working in hundreds of languages around the world.[19] Through this work, Nida became the pioneer and primary advocate of the theory of dynamic equivalence translation, an approach that has been used to translate the Bible into many obscure languages in many nations of the world.

Although I will disagree with Nida's theory of dynamic equivalence in the following paragraphs, it is important that I first express appreciation to Nida for his immense contributions to the translation of the Bible into many hundreds of obscure languages in many remote parts of the world. In addition, his dynamic equivalence theory no doubt provided a helpful correction to the overly literal views that had led, for example, to the 1901 American Standard Version, with its difficult sentence structure that reflected the word order of the original languages but yielded very awkward, unnatural English. For these things I do have appreciation. However, as I have explained in the preceding pages, it seems to me that there are significant weaknesses in dynamic equivalence theory that also need to be understood.

In a 2002 interview in *Christianity Today,* Nida explained that his undergraduate training at UCLA influenced his own view of translation:

> "When I was at the University of California, Los Angeles, our professors would never let us translate literally. They said, 'We want to know the meaning. We don't want to know just the words.'"

Then, in explaining why new translators who come to his training conferences often resist the theory of dynamic equivalence, Nida says,

> "They can accept it intellectually but not emotionally because they've grown up worshiping words more than worshiping God. . . . This 'word worship' helps people to have confidence, but they don't understand the text. And as long as they worship words, instead of worshiping God as revealed in Jesus Christ, they feel safe."[20]

---

[19] Biographical information about Eugene Nida was taken from www.nidainstitute.org July 9, 2005.
[20] Eugene Nida, interview by David Neff, "Meaning-full Translations: The World's Most Influential Bible Translator, Eugene Nida, Is Weary of 'Word Worship,'" *Christianity Today,* October 7, 2002, 46.

So Nida seems to be saying that he developed his theory of translation from the teaching of his UCLA professors. But he gives no evidence of being influenced by the teaching of the Bible about the importance of its own words. I am not sure that the translation theories of certain secular professors provide an obviously superior foundation for translation, rather than the statements of the Bible about its own words. Nor is it clear that all linguistics experts agree with Nida's former UCLA professors that essentially literal translation is an improper goal: see, for example, the comments (in another context) of Valerie Becker Makkai, past president of the Linguistic Association of Canada and the U.S., regarding the importance of accurately translating the very words of the Bible.[21]

As for Nida's criticism that those who favor word-for-word translation are guilty of "word worship" rather than worshiping God, it is simply a distorted caricature. No supporters of essentially literal translation put a Bible in front of the church and sing to it, "O Bible, we worship you! O words of the Bible, we praise you! O Bible words, please hear our prayers!" That is foolishness, and Nida's critique misrepresents the thoughtful, sincere, intellectually sound approaches to essentially literal translation that scholars have understood for centuries.

In *The Theory and Practice of Translation*,[22] Nida and Charles Taber explain their views more fully. They explain that translators need

> a shift in some of the attitudes which tend to place the source languages on a theological pedestal and to bow down before them in blind submission. . . .
> Greek and Hebrew are just "languages," with all the excellencies and liabilities that every language tends to have. They are neither the languages of heaven nor the speech of the Holy Spirit.[23]

But if Nida thinks that the Greek and Hebrew words of the original manuscripts of the Bible are not the "speech of the Holy Spirit," then

---

[21] Valerie Becker Makkai, "Foreword," in Vern Poythress and Wayne Grudem, *The TNIV and the Gender-Neutral Bible Controversy* (Nashville: Broadman & Holman, 2004), xix-xxv.
[22] Eugene Nida and Charles Taber, *The Theory and Practice of Translation* (Leiden and Boston: Brill, 2003; first published 1969).
[23] Ibid., 3, 6.

it makes sense that he would not see the need to preserve and translate the meaning of every word. If they are not God's words, but merely human words, then the individual words are not so important.

For Nida, then, the goal of translation is not being faithful to the meaning of the *original text,* but rather the goal is to bring about a proper *response* from the reader. When Nida evaluates a translation, his primary reference point is not the words of the original text but rather the degree to which modern readers will understand the translation. This is evident in the following comments:

> The new focus, however, has shifted from the form of the message to the response of the receptor. Therefore, what one must determine is the response of the receptor to the translated message. This response must then be compared with the way in which the original receptors presumably reacted to the message when it was given in its original setting. . . .
>
> Correctness [of a translation] must be determined by the extent to which the average reader for which a translation is intended will be likely to understand it correctly. Moreover, we are not concerned merely with the possibility of his understanding correctly, but with the overwhelming likelihood of it. In other words, we are not content merely to translate so that the average receptor is likely to understand the message; rather we aim to make certain that such a person is very unlikely to misunderstand it.[24]

> To measure dynamic equivalence we can only rightly compare the equivalence of response, rather than the degree of agreement between the original source and the later receptors, for we cannot presume that the source was writing for this "unknown audience." . . .
>
> Dynamic equivalence is therefore to be defined in terms of the degree to which the receptors of the message in the receptor language respond to it in substantially the same manner as the receptors in the source language.[25]

In actual practice the "average reader" for Nida is primarily a non-Christian reader, for he explains, "the Scriptures must be intelli-

---

[24] Ibid., 1.
[25] Ibid., 23-24.

gible to non-Christians, and if they are, they will also be intelligible to Christians."[26]

While I agree that translators should weigh heavily the ability of ordinary readers to understand a translation, I do not think that reader response should be the primary criterion for good translation. Rather, the primary criterion should be faithfulness to the words of the original text, representing their meaning accurately in English (or another language) even if at times that means that the meaning is difficult to understand or requires some effort on the part of the reader.

Nida wants a Bible in which it is certain that an average reader "is very unlikely to misunderstand it." In practice that means a Bible with simple vocabulary, simple, short sentences, and thousands of verses that state the main idea clearly but leave out details and complexities of meaning that are there in the original Greek or Hebrew text. But what if the Bible is not that simple a book, and what if the Bible was not that simple even when its various books were first written? What if many parts of it were difficult to understand even for the original readers?

What if God gave us a Bible that was not easy to understand in every place? What if he gave us a Bible that had layers and depths of meaning that an "average reader" who is a non-Christian will simply not comprehend on first or second reading, and that Christians themselves will only understand after repeated study, reflection, and meditation? What if God gave us a Bible that contains wisdom that is "not a wisdom of this age, or of the rulers of this age," but is "a secret and hidden wisdom of God, which God decreed before the ages for our glory," a wisdom that "none of the rulers of this age understood" (1 Cor. 2:6-8, ESV)? Is it then right to simplify or remove everything that we think some average readers will find difficult?

Nida's primary emphasis on reader understandability neglects the fact that the Bible has depths and richness of meaning that can never be fully understood by any person in one lifetime. That is because it is the speech not only of men but also of God, and divine authorship is fully operative in every part of it (2 Tim. 3:16; 2 Pet. 1:20-21). Divine wisdom is reflected in every detail of it, and this is a wisdom beyond all of

---

[26] Ibid., 31.

our ability to fully understand or exhaust. Even Peter the apostle admits that there are some things in Paul's epistles "hard to understand" (2 Pet. 3:16), and he recognizes that the Old Testament prophets themselves did not always understand completely the meaning of their own writings as they were guided by the Holy Spirit (1 Pet. 1:10-12). So when Nida places such priority on the readers and hearers of Scripture as opposed to placing primary emphasis on faithfulness to the original text of Scripture, he seems to misunderstand the nature of Scripture as the product of the infinite mind of God our Creator.

Our goal should not be just to produce a simplified, easy-to-understand translation that uses only common contemporary forms of speech, that is nearly impossible for anyone to misunderstand, and that leaves out thousands upon thousands of details of meaning that are there in the text in the original Hebrew and Greek. Our goal rather should be to produce a translation that brings over into English as much of the meaning of the original text as possible within the constraints of good English today. Some parts of such a translation will be clear and easy for almost anyone to understand. Other parts will be more complex and more challenging to contemporary readers, just as they no doubt were to the original recipients of some of Paul's epistles when they first received and read them as native speakers of Greek. Our final standard of good translation should be faithfulness to the original text, not just easy understandability by average non-Christian readers.

VIII. CONCLUSION

Our views about the proper goal of a Bible translation should be determined primarily by the teachings of the Bible about its own character and the nature of its words, not by some secular linguistic theories, and not by our estimates of how much or how little an average non-Christian reader will understand.

When dynamic equivalence translations again and again leave out the meaning of words that are there in the original Hebrew and Greek texts, and when they again and again add meanings that have no basis in the words of the original texts, they do not seem to me to be placing adequate emphasis on all the words of Scripture as the very words of God. By contrast, essentially literal translations seek to translate faithfully the contextually understood meanings of every word in the original texts. Therefore it seems to me that belief in the plenary inspiration of Scripture—the idea that all the words of Scripture are the words of God—strongly favors essentially literal translation of the Bible, and seriously calls into question the theory of dynamic equivalence translation.

2

FIVE MYTHS ABOUT ESSENTIALLY LITERAL BIBLE TRANSLATION

LELAND RYKEN

THERE CAN BE NO DOUBT that we have entered an era of renewed debate about translation theory and practice. The practitioners of dynamic equivalence, after having had the playing field pretty much to themselves for half a century, now find their hegemony challenged by advocates of essentially literal translation theory. When D. A. Carson recently revised an essay that he published nearly two decades earlier on translation theory and practice, one of three developments that he cited as having arrived on the scene between his two essays was "the rise of linguistic conservatism."[1]

The challenge posed by linguistic conservatism to dynamic equivalence has elicited a predictable counter movement in which advocates of dynamic equivalence have defended their cherished views and translations against the criticisms that have been made against them. As the defenders of dynamic equivalence have made their counterarguments, they have evolved a list of charges against the theory and practice of essentially literal translation. I propose to examine five common charges, which, because of my own commitment to essentially literal translation, I will call myths or fallacies.

---

[1] D. A. Carson, "The Limits of Functional Equivalence in Bible Translation—and Other Limits, Too," in *The Challenge of Bible Translation*, Glen G. Scorgie et al., eds. (Grand Rapids, Mich.: Zondervan, 2003), 66.

A few preliminary definitions will prove helpful. "Essentially literal" does not mean totally literal. It means that a translation strives to find the English word or combination of words that most accurately corresponds to the words of the original text. It does not mean translating the original in a way that makes no sense in English. Furthermore, retaining the syntax of the original, though not an irrelevant consideration, is nonetheless not a high priority, inasmuch as Hebrew and Greek syntax is so different from English syntax.

The most common criticism that has been voiced against the ESV, since its publication in 2001, is that it violates its own philosophy in not being totally literal and not retaining the syntax of the original Hebrew and Greek. The criticism is frivolous and wide of the mark, inasmuch as no essentially literal translation claims to be completely literal, least of all in regard to syntax. The formula "essentially literal" means what it says; it does not mean "completely literal."

I need to clarify secondly that my subject in this chapter is English Bible translation. I am not expert to consider the exigencies of translating the Bible into newly emerging or recently codified written languages. I will note in passing that in the wake of my book *The Word of God in English: Criteria for Excellence in Bible Translation* (Crossway, 2002), I have found a sympathetic response from many missionary-translators who are working with new languages, despite the fact that it was this branch of translation that gave rise to dynamic equivalence as the dominant modern theory of translation.

MYTH #1: ADVOCATES OF ESSENTIALLY LITERAL TRANSLATION ARE GUILTY OF WORD WORSHIP AND IDOLATRY.

When I was writing my book on Bible translation, I naturally found it useful to seek guidance from colleagues at Wheaton College who are expert in the original languages of the Bible, an expertise that I myself lack. In one exchange, a colleague who is never-failing in his helpfulness to me, even though he is a thoroughgoing advocate of dynamic translation, wrote in an email, "I am reluctant to sacrifice meaning to the idol of word-for-word correspondence." I thought that the word *idol* was a rather strong word but did not pursue the matter.

A month or two later *Christianity Today* carried an interview with Eugene Nida.[2] There, staring at me from the page, was this statement of put-down of literal translation: "This 'word worship' helps people to have confidence, but they don't understand the text. And as long as they worship words, instead of worshiping God as revealed in Jesus Christ, they feel safe."[3] Lest we think that this was a slip of the tongue in an unguarded moment, elsewhere in the interview I found the same formula: "When we bring together a group of folks who want to be translators, it takes a month to get them willing to make sense intellectually. It takes another two weeks to make them willing to do it emotionally. They can accept it intellectually but not emotionally because they've grown up worshiping words more than worshiping God."[4]

Questions arise at this point. What makes it either more or less idolatrous to assign priority to the words of the original as distinct from the ideas or meaning? All translation theorists assign priority to *something*. Nida, for example, evolved the rule that gave "the priority of the needs of the audience over the forms of language," and further decreed that "the use of language by persons twenty-five to thirty years of age has priority over the language of the older people or of children," and that "in certain situations the speech of women should have priority over the speech of men."[5] While I believe that this ascribes an unwarranted and dangerous priority to the audience, surely it would be a strange polemical maneuver for me to say that Nida has made an idol of that audience.

As an advocate of linguistic conservatism, by which I mean that an English translation should preserve as much as possible of the very words of the original, I feel that I am on very good grounds, inasmuch as the Bible itself ascribes inspiration to the very words of Scripture. I offer the following as a very brief list of passages that assign primacy to the words of Scripture rather than the thoughts:

> Then the Lord put out his hand and touched my mouth. And the Lord said to me, "Behold, I have put my words in your mouth" (Jer. 1:9, ESV).

[2] Eugene Nida, "Meaning-full Translations: The World's Most Influential Bible Translator, Eugene Nida, Is Weary of 'Word Worship,'" *Christianity Today*, October 7, 2002: 46-49.
[3] Ibid., 46.
[4] Ibid.
[5] Eugene A. Nida and Charles R. Taber, *The Theory and Practice of Translation* (Leiden: Brill, 1969), 32.

And we impart this in words not taught by human wisdom but taught by the Spirit (1 Cor. 2:13, ESV).

Now the promises were made to Abraham and to his offspring. It does not say, "And to offsprings," referring to many, but referring to one, "And to your offspring," who is Christ (Gal. 3:16, ESV).

"The words that I have spoken to you are spirit and life" (John 6:63, ESV).

Regarding the last passage, Martin Luther correctly noted, "Christ did not say of His thoughts, but of His words, that they are spirit and life."[6]

Let me say in passing that the debate over translation needs to be conducted in a principled way. Advocates of the rival theory to one's own might fairly be viewed as intellectual *opponents,* but we should not resort to charges of *idolatry.* My plea for respect and humility carries over into a second myth regarding essentially literal translation theory and practice.

MYTH #2: ESSENTIALLY LITERAL TRANSLATION THEORY AND PRACTICE ARE NAIVE.

D. A. Carson responds to a critic of the NIV with such phrases as "hopelessly naive" and guilty of "astonishing naivete."[7] Ronald Youngblood speaks of "the incredibly naive statements made in more than one recent volume on translation theory."[8] An anonymous Amazon.com reviewer of my book spoke of "the naive assumption that words are the sole component of meaning," which, incidentally, is not the position I embrace.

What does the common charge of naivete mean? Is it more than a put-down of an intellectual opponent? What is the opposite of naive? The most obvious answer is that the opposite of being naive is to be sophisticated, but what, then, are the things that make up sophistication? Are we talking about a difference between simple and complex? Or between plainly stated versus couched in the specialized vocabulary and concep-

[6] Martin Luther, quoted in René Paché, *The Inspiration and Authority of Scripture,* trans. Helen I. Needham (Chicago: Moody, 1969), 75.
[7] Carson, "Limits of Functional Equivalence," 73.
[8] Ronald Youngblood, "Translation versus Transliteration: The Triumph of Clarity over Opacity," address at the 2003 annual meeting of the Evangelical Theological Society, accessed online.

tual framework of a discipline such as linguistics? Does naive mean "ignorant, uninformed, uneducated, and even unintelligent?" These questions are not easily answered, leading me to question whether the word *naive* is the right term to use. Nonetheless, since the discussion has been framed in terms of naivete, I have decided to use the word that has gained currency among those who wish to disparage essentially literal translation.

Let me begin by saying that the goal in Bible translation is truth. If the truth is what some would call naive, then naivete is what we want. Conversely, sophistication is not a desirable trait if it lacks truth. With that proviso in place, I can think of ways in which essentially literal translation is a naive procedure, and I can think of more ways in which dynamic equivalence is naive.

First, essentially literal translation is a simple theory in the sense that it has not based itself on complicated linguistic theory. To me, this is a strength, not a weakness. I believe that English Bible translation took a wrong turn when it was taken over by linguists who trade in a highly specialized technical vocabulary. I am skeptical of a discipline that is encrusted in as highly technical and obscure a vocabulary as linguistics is. For me, essentially literal translation begets confidence partly because it is a commonsense and simple approach.

Furthermore, the fact that dynamic equivalence *theory* has been surrounded by a complex linguistic framework has obscured the simplicity of its actual *practice*. When a translation renders Matthew 5:3—"blessed are the poor in spirit"—as "you're blessed when you're at the end of your rope" (MESSAGE), the principle at work is simple, namely, that old and familiar versions of a passage need to be enlivened by being rendered into contemporary colloquialisms.

When a translation renders Psalm 1:1—"who walks not in the counsel of the wicked"—as "who reject the advice of evil men" (GNB), the principle involved is simple: in the words of Eugene Nida himself, the metaphoric statement in the original "is not understood" by modern readers, so the metaphor must be replaced by plain statement.[9]

Again, when a translation renders Ecclesiastes 9:8—"Let your garments be always white. Let not oil be lacking on your head"—as, "Wear fine clothes, with a dash of cologne!" (NLT), the principle underlying the

---

[9] Eugene A. Nida, *Good News for Everyone* (Waco, Tex: Word, 1977), 10.

translation is simple, namely, that references to ancient customs in the world of the biblical text should be modernized by being rendered into current customs. When a translation renders John 6:27—"on him God the Father has set his seal"—as "seal of approval" (NIV) or "seal of his authority" (REB), no complicated linguistic principle is involved; the principle involved is the simple one of mingling commentary with translation to guide the reader into accepting a translation committee's preferred interpretation of the passage.

To summarize: if the concept of naivete is defined as meaning simple rather than complex and free from overt influence of linguistic theory, then essentially literal translation can be accurately characterized in this way. But dynamic equivalence *practice* is no less naive in its actual procedures (as distinct from the technical linguistic scaffolding with which dynamic equivalence *theory* is typically surrounded).

A second way in which essentially literal translation is simple in conception and therefore, in the neutral sense of the term, naive, is in its refusal to add the functions of interpretation, exegesis, and editing to the task of translation. Dynamic equivalence translators regularly resort to the following practices, all of which move beyond translation of the passage into activities that in other areas of life we ascribe to the exegete, the editor, and the social reformer:

- changing vocabulary that is considered difficult or old-fashioned into vocabulary that is contemporary or colloquial;
- changing figurative language into non-figurative language;
- changing a statement that the translator considers not immediately understandable into a statement that uses different words from the source to match what the translator regards as fitting the needs of a contemporary reader;
- eliminating words that are regarded as technical theological terms and replacing them with plain, non-technical language;
- reducing the vocabulary level of the source;
- changing gender references to match the editor's ideas on proper language for gender in our own culture.

Essentially literal translation is virtually devoid of these maneuvers, except where the original biblical text makes no sense when translated literally and therefore requires changing in order to make sense in English. By conceiving the task of translation in strict or narrow terms rather than the latitudinarian terms that produce the practices I have listed, essentially literal translation is simple and in that sense naive. So much the better for it. Dynamic equivalence translations are actually hybrids, combining features of a translation, a commentary, and a text edited to meet the translators' preferences for a given audience.

If the charge of naivete is actually a code language to belittle translators' level of expertise and knowledge of the original text of the Bible, then the designation must be decisively rejected. The translation committees that produce dynamic equivalence English Bibles are not more educated than the committees that produce essentially literal translations.

Furthermore, since the charge of naivete is in part an attempt to marginalize adherents of essentially literal translation as an inconsequential segment of the English translation scene, it is important to set the record straight in this regard. Even though new English translations have been dominated by dynamic equivalence, the English Bibles actually in use have been pretty evenly divided between literal and free translations. And in terms of the history of English Bible translation, dynamic equivalence is almost wholly a modern phenomenon. No major English translation was dominated by dynamic equivalence until the mid-twentieth century, and in this regard appeals to the Wycliffe translation of the fourteenth century and occasional freedoms that Tyndale took are irrelevant to the discourse. If Tyndale gave us anomalies like claiming that Paul sailed from Philippi after the Easter holidays, he also coined words like *intercession* and *atonement* in order to express the theological content of the original. In terms of the history of English Bible translation, therefore, essentially literal translation is the dominant tradition, not a lightweight view held by a few ignorant people.

I have asserted two ways in which essentially literal translation is simple or naive, namely, in its freedom from specialized linguistic scaffolding and in its refusal to move beyond translation to functions ordinarily assigned to commentators and editors. I have also noted one way in which the term is inappropriate, namely, as a put-down of the expertise of those who engage in essentially literal translation. I turn next to areas in which I believe that dynamic equivalence theory and practice are naive, in contrast to essentially literal translation theory and practice.

To begin, non-literal translations operate on the premise of a naive or minimally educated reader. Having accepted a grade school reading level as the norm, some translation committees then produce simplified Bibles for an uneducated or lowest common denominator readership. Sometimes the prefaces of translations make explicit that the translators have aimed to produce a simplified Bible. One preface links "the average reader of modern English" with "the reading level of a junior high student" (NLT). Another "easy reading" translation claims an English vocabulary of 3,000 words (The Simplified Bible). A friend of mine who espouses dynamic equivalence recently posed the issue in terms of whether a translation should be oriented toward a college educated person or "the sixth-grade dropout in the pew."

There are more things than reading level and vocabulary that make up the assumption of a naive audience for the Bible. Some translations operate on the premise that readers should not be expected to handle theological or technical terminology. One translator claimed that the Good News Bible was designed for the "unsophisticated" or "average" reader who would be grateful for "being delivered from theological subtleties."[10] A translator who worked on the NEB claimed that it was intended for an audience with minimal acquaintance with the Bible—people, for example, "who do not go to church."[11] The CEV is committed to "the avoidance of traditionally theological language and words like 'atonement', 'redemption', 'righteousness' and 'sanctification'."[12]

Further assumptions about modern readers fill out the picture of what I call a naive readership. Dynamic equivalence translations regularly assume that contemporary readers struggle with figurative language, so that, in the words of one translation, "at times we have chosen to translate or illuminate the metaphor" (NLT). Incidentally, translating the metaphor is exactly what equivalence translations do *not* do; they do not translate the metaphor but remove it from sight. Not only is figurative language said to be beyond the ability of modern readers, but so is the ability to enter the ancientness and foreignness of the biblical

---

[10] Cited in Stephen Prickett, *Words and the Word: Language, Poetics and Biblical Interpretation* (Cambridge: Cambridge University Press, 1986), 6.

[11] C. H. Dodd, quoted in T. S. Eliot, review of the NEB, in *The New English Bible Reviewed,* ed. Dennis Nineham (London: Epworth, 1965), 100.

[12] Alec Gilmore, *A Dictionary of the English Bible and Its Origins* (Sheffield, UK: Sheffield Academic Press, 2000), 54.

world. In the preface to the NIV, we read that the translators based two of their renderings on the premise that "for most readers today the phrases 'the LORD of hosts' and 'God of hosts' have little meaning." An unstated and perhaps unrecognized assumption in all this is that readers cannot be educated beyond their current abilities—to me a naive and untenable premise. If this were not the operating premise, translation committees would not fix their translation at a lowest common denominator of reading ability and comprehension. In effect, "easy reading" translations *ensure* that readers will remain at a naive level of comprehension, even if the translators would disavow that this is their aim.

This, then, is one way in which dynamic equivalence translations are naive: the translators producing them assume an audience with minimal linguistic and theological ability and then produce a translation adapted to the assumed needs of that audience. Essentially literal translations are not naive in this sense. They expect from their readers what we as a society expect of educated adults and even bright teenagers in other areas of life. The reply to the charge of elitism is simple: essentially literal translations make the Bible neither more nor less difficult than it was in the original. Faithfulness to the original is the goal of essentially literal translation; catering to the assumed wants and needs of the modern reader is the goal of dynamic equivalence translations.

A second area in which dynamic equivalence is naive is its refusal to make a valid distinction between what the original says and what the translator believes that it means. I want to begin by acknowledging that this is a complex subject on which it is difficult to discover accurate terminology by which to name the issues.

Of course an English translation does not repeat the exact words of the original text; it is a translation. But the usual ploy of dynamic equivalence advocates is to say, "See—no translation preserves the language of the original," a maneuver that misrepresents the situation. There remains a demonstrable difference between English translations that give us the equivalent English word and English translations that do not give us the equivalent English word, either by changing the words of the original or by adding words that are not present in the original. We need *some* language by which to name the difference between a translation that reads "Your hair is like a flock of goats / leaping down the slopes of Gilead" (Song 4:1, ESV) and a translation that reads "Your hair falls in waves, like flocks of goats frisking across the slopes of Gilead" (NLT).

Much of the time what a translated word or phrase says and what the translator believes that it means are identical, and in these instances essentially literal and dynamic equivalence translations are likely to produce identical or similar translations. In these cases, there is no good reason for dynamic equivalence translations not to reproduce in English what the original says, since the word-for-word correspondence is clear in English. But when a dynamic equivalence translation goes beyond a word-for-word correspondence to something more interpretive (in effect a substitution for what the original says), the old distinction between what a text says and what it means remains valid.

For example, what 1 Thessalonians 2:12 *says* is, "Walk in a manner worthy of God." That is indisputable. The translation "live in a manner worthy of God" is one version of what it *means*. In such an instance, we can, indeed, distinguish between these two. James 1:18 says "that we should be a kind of firstfruits of his creation." All of the following translations omit what the clause *says* (with its metaphor of firstfruits) and offer an interpretation of what it *means:* "he wanted us to be his own special people" (CEV); "showing us off as the crown of all his creatures" (MESSAGE); "that we should have first place among all his creatures" (GNB).

In these instances, it is demonstrably untrue that we cannot differentiate between translations that preserve what the text says and those that substitute a preferred understanding of what the text means. The naivete lies with those who deny the difference.

As for the repercussions of moving from what the original says to what the translator believes that it means in the process of translation, Ray Van Leeuwen correctly says, "It is hard to know what the Bible *means* when we are uncertain about what it *says*. . . . The problem with [functionally equivalent] translations . . . is that they prevent the reader from inferring biblical *meaning* because they change what the Bible *said*."[13]

Yet another point on which dynamic equivalence translations are naive relates to the reductionistic tendencies of dynamic equivalence

---

[13] Raymond C. Van Leeuwen, "We Really Do Need Another Bible Translation," *Christianity Today*, October 22, 2001, 30.

translations. Essentially literal translations have as a high goal to preserve the full exegetical potential of the original biblical text. This means retaining ambiguities and multiple meanings in a biblical statement. It also means leaving figurative language to the interpretive decision of the reader instead of interspersing interpretive commentary in the text or actually replacing what is in the original text with something else (sometimes with an entirely new metaphor!). By contrast, the general tendency of dynamically equivalent translations is to eliminate ambiguity, interpret figurative language, and produce a one-dimensional Bible in which a firm editorial hand has attempted to guide readers into the "right" interpretation and guard against incorrect interpretation.

Let me cite some random specimens. "The love of Christ constrains us," says 2 Corinthians 5:14 (RSV, NASB, REB, JB, ESV). Does this mean "our love for Christ" or "Christ's love for us"? Probably both, but in any case the original leaves the door open to both interpretations. One-dimensional, simplified translations make a preemptive interpretive strike, translating the statement as "Christ's love" (NIV, CEV, NLT).

Psalm 90:12 states, "So teach us to number our days" ("number our days aright," NIV). Numbering our days is a difficult image that requires interpretation and does not carry its meaning on the surface. Does it mean to ponder or pay close attention to, as we do when we count ("number") objects? Does the image of numbering mean to tally up as our days unfold, with the implied meaning of looking back and making sense of our past days? Does numbering one's days mean counting them with a view toward seeing how few they are? Is the imagery of numbering our days a code word for valuing our days? Is it a code word for *using* our days appropriately? Is this statement a continuation of the negative view of time that has prevailed up to this point in the psalm, or is it a positive and hopeful *antidote* to the melancholy view of time's passing that has preceded in the psalm?

All of these interpretations have been validly argued by the commentators. An essentially literal translation keeps the door open to all valid interpretations simply by retaining the language of the original: "teach us to number our days." Translators who do not want to pass on the ambiguity or potentially multiple meanings to their readers resolve the issue by narrowing and simplifying the text to a single meaning: "so make us know how few are our days" (REB); "teach us how short our life is" (GNB); "teach us to make the most of our time" (NLT). All of these interpretations are possible, but all of the translations just quoted reduce the options to just one possibility. In a word, they simplify, whereas translations that render the verse literally preserve the full richness and exegetical potential of the text.

The people who are placed in the ultimate position of naivete are, of course, the readers of a dynamic equivalence translation. These readers have no clue as to what has been removed from sight, or what interpretive decisions have been made for them by the translation committee. The typical reader operates on the premise that what Psalm 90:12 says is (for example) "teach us how short our life is," oblivious to the fact that the original uses a metaphor and that, furthermore, this metaphor has been interpreted in half a dozen legitimate ways.

In the urge to relieve allegedly inexpert readers from the need to make interpretive decisions, and to guard readers from misinterpretation, dynamic equivalence translators overlook one important thing: in the overwhelming number of instances where these translators believe that they need to change, explain, or clarify the original, *the original authors could have said it that way and chose not to.* The psalmist had the linguistic resources to say (in Ps. 78:33) that God ended the days of the wicked "in futility" (NIV) or "in emptiness" (REB) or "in failure" (NLT) instead of saying that "their days vanish like a breath" (RSV, ESV, NRSV). At the heart of the dynamic equivalence experiment is the attempt to fix the assumed inadequacies of the Bible for modern readers. This maneuver is not an example of sophistication as opposed to the naivete; it is instead an unwarranted affront to the original authors (an extension of the "what the author was *trying* to say" fallacy that has become so prevalent).

A final point on which I find dynamic equivalence naive is its assumption that we can retain the meaning of the original text without retaining its precise words. Dynamic equivalence theorists support their practice with technical linguistic scaffolding. I will buttress my theory with a bit of *literary* theory.

A basic principle of modern literary theory is that, in the words of one influential twentieth-century literary critic, "Form *is* meaning."[14] Or

---

[14] Cleanth Brooks, "The Formalist Critic," in *The Modern Critical Spectrum,* Gerald Jay Goldberg and Nancy M. Goldberg, eds. (Englewood Cliffs, N. J.: Prentice-Hall, 1962), 1.

we might invoke Marshall McLuhan's famous formula that "the medium is the message." By contrast, Eugene Nida and Charles Taber naively and dismissively posit that "words are merely vehicles for ideas."[15] This position was subsequently echoed by dynamic equivalence advocates John Beekman and John Callow when they asserted that "the forms are simply a 'vehicle' with which to get the message across to the recipients."[16] Words are "merely" and "simply" a vehicle. This is a naive view of language that is echoed by Mark Strauss in his dismissive view of words as "arbitrary and conventional symbols used to signify meaning."[17] At the heart of the disagreement between the rival theories of translation lies the disagreement about the nature and primacy of words in language communication.

Even Strauss' designation "meaning-based translation" represents an elementary failure in logic by overlooking that meaning is based on something that is precedent, namely, words. There *is* no meaning without words; if we change the words, we change the meaning. Similarly naive is Nida's answer to the question, "What units of written texts carry the most meaning?" Nida's reply: "The phrase."[18] The obvious question that this raises is, Of what do phrases consist? They consist of words.

The omission of the concept of words in the prefaces to dynamic equivalence translations, in contrast to the prefaces of essentially literal translations, signals what to me is a naive attempt to bypass the thing from which meaning arises. "*Meaning* not *form* is the goal of Bible translation," writes Strauss.[19] My reply is that the goal is meaning *through* or *based on* form.

I need to guard against a potential misunderstanding at this point. I agree with translators (including advocates of dynamic equivalence) who claim that the ultimate goal of translation is the clear communication of the Bible's meaning. Meaning is, indeed, the final goal. Conversely, form for the sake of form is *not* the goal. The fallacy, though, is in thinking that we can get the meaning correct if we

---

[15] Nida and Taber, *Theory and Practice of Translation,* 13.

[16] John Beekman and John Callow, *Translating the Word of God* (Grand Rapids, Mich.: Zondervan, 1974), 25.

[17] Mark L. Strauss, "Form, Function, and the 'Literal Meaning' Fallacy in Bible Translation," address at the 2003 annual meeting of the Evangelical Theological Society, accessed online.

[18] Nida, "Meaning-full Translations," 48.

[19] Strauss, accessed online.

do not retain the words of the original—if we remove from sight references to "numbering" our days or having our days "vanish like a breath."

MYTH #3: ESSENTIALLY LITERAL TRANSLATION IS NO MORE THAN TRANSCRIPTION OR TRANSLITERATION.

In a review of my book, Mark Strauss claimed that I "forget that [I am] talking about translation rather than transcription."[20] Ronald Youngblood entitled his address defending dynamic equivalence "Translation versus Transliteration: The Triumph of Clarity over Opacity." Quite apart from such scholarly sources, I have found the claim that literal translation is no more than transcription to be a common put-down.

The claim is easily tested. A transcription of Psalm 32:1 would read,

Blessedness of forgiven of transgression, covered of sin.

Which of the following English Bible versions are transcriptions?

Oh, what joy for those whose rebellion is forgiven, whose sin is put out of sight! (NLT).

How blessed is he whose transgression is forgiven, Whose sin is covered (NASB).

Happy are those whose sins are forgiven, whose wrongs are pardoned (GNB).

Blessed is the one whose transgression is forgiven, whose sin is covered (ESV).

Count yourself lucky, how happy you must be—you get a fresh start, your slate's wiped clean (MESSAGE).

---

[20] Mark Strauss, review of *The Word of God in English,* by Leland Ryken, *Journal of the Evangelical Theological Society* 46 (2003): 739.

According to the allegation commonly raised against essentially literal translations, two of the five versions that I quoted are transliterations, while the others are translations. The claim is obviously false.

To take a New Testament instance, a transcription of 2 Timothy 1:13 would read,

> pattern of sound words of which from me you heard in faith and love the in Christ Jesus.

Which of the following English renderings are transliterations or transcriptions?

> What you heard from me, keep as the pattern of sound teaching, with faith and love in Christ Jesus (NIV).

> Hold firmly to the true words that I taught you, as the example for you to follow, and remain in the faith and love that are ours in union with Christ Jesus (GNB).

> Follow the pattern of the sound words that you have heard from me, in the faith and love that are in Christ Jesus (ESV).

> Hold on to the pattern of right teaching you learned from me. And remember to live in the faith and love that you have in Christ Jesus (NLT).

It is obvious that *none* of these English translations is a transliteration or transcription. The charge that essentially literal translations are mere transcriptions should be labeled for what it is—frivolous and irresponsible.

MYTH #4: ESSENTIALLY LITERAL TRANSLATORS FAIL TO UNDERSTAND THAT ALL TRANSLATION IS INTERPRETATION.

Essentially literal translators do not deny that there is a sense in which all translation is interpretation. They are simply more discriminating than dynamic equivalence translators in applying the principle. Let me say in passing that I know of no principle of translation that has been more abused than this favorite motto of dynamic equivalence translators.

There is one sense—and in my view only one sense—in which the commonly invoked cliché is accurate. All translation requires linguistic or lexical interpretation of what word in the receptor language best expresses the meaning of the word in the source language. Were the Israelites led through the desert or the wilderness? Translation requires continuous interpretive decisions at this linguistic level. For all the disparagement of the idea that good translation involves, at some level, a word-for-word correspondence, I myself believe that virtually all words in the original Old and New Testaments do have a corresponding English word or combination of words by which to express the words of the original.

All translation is lexical interpretation, but this is the least of what excites dynamic equivalence advocates. In fact, they seem often to be impatient with finding the right corresponding word, but eager to interpret the meaning of the passage or phrase for the ignorant reader of the Bible on the basis of allegedly superior information. I believe that it is naive not to differentiate between types of interpretation in regard to modern translation practices. The translation of Psalm 23:5b as "you anoint my head with oil" is qualitatively different from the rendering "you welcome me as an honored guest" (GNB). The first of these is linguistic interpretation, yielding the English words that most accurately express the lexical meaning of the Hebrew words and preserving the metaphor of anointing of the head. The second translation actually bypasses linguistic interpretation in the final translation and resorts to interpretation of the conceptual meaning.

In this regard I want to defend what I did in the early chapters of my book on English Bible translation when I surveyed situations in everyday life where we regard as crucial the preservation of the exact words of a speaker or writer when transmitting a communication. Examples included legal documents, eyewitness accounts, recipes, love letters, newspaper interviews, and quotations in research papers. Dynamic equivalence advocates claim that because my examples come from English language texts they are irrelevant to translation (an anonymous reviewer of my book on the Amazon website claimed that I mixed apples and oranges). These critics are wrong, for two reasons.

First, in the overwhelming preponderance of cases where dynamic equivalence translations abandon adherence to the actual words of the original, there is absolutely nothing in the translation process that *requires* the liberties that have been taken. Dynamic equivalence translators use the translation process as the occasion for license, as they do things with the original text that we do not allow with texts in their native language. There is nothing in the translation process that requires (or, according to my theory, condones) rendering Psalm 87:7b—"all my springs are in you" (ESV; NIV, "all my fountains are in you")—as "the source of my life is in Jerusalem" (NLT) or "in Zion is the source of all our blessings" (GNB). The most obvious characteristic of dynamic equivalence translators is that they use the process of translation as the occasion to do things with texts that they themselves would not condone in texts (including ones that they themselves write) as they exist in their own language.

Second, when I adduce examples from everyday life in which we regard the exact wording as crucial, the principle involved has nothing to do per se with translation. It has to do rather with the ethical obligations that any intermediary owes to both an author and a recipient when transmitting a communication from a source to a receptor. I believe that the rules are the same for texts in their original language as they are for a language into which they are translated, namely, preservation of the way in which the original expressed its content in as full a manner as possible.

MYTH #5: ESSENTIALLY LITERAL TRANSLATIONS ARE OBSCURE AND OPAQUE.

Several ideas ordinarily cluster around the charge of obscurity. One is the assumption that whenever an English translation is difficult or unclear, the fault can be assumed to lie with the translation and its philosophy rather than being a property of the original biblical text. Related to this is the assumption that when a colloquial or modernized translation is judged by reading tests to be more easily grasped by the population at large, this means that translations that require a higher reading level are obscure.

It is my belief that all modern translations are clear and readable. This is not to deny that some modern translations are accessible to a lower reading level than traditional translations are. Not only has readability been elevated to a status all out of proportion to its legitimate place, but it has also been misrepresented. I have moved among people for whom readability is apparently the primary aim of English Bible translation, an error reinforced by advertising for what I will call "easy reading Bibles." I will state my critique of the readability fallacy very succinctly: what good is readability if what the reader reads is not what the original text of the Bible says? If it is not what the original text says, a so-called readable translation has actually *removed* the Bible from a reader, not, as is claimed, brought the Bible close to the reader.

The implication that modern readers need special consideration of their weaknesses as readers is written right into the prefaces of some translations—prefaces, may I note, that are written in sophisticated prose far removed from the reading level to which the translation itself has been slanted. One preface claims that "metaphorical language is often difficult for contemporary readers to understand" (NLT). Another preface states that "ancient customs are often unfamiliar to modern readers" (NCV). By thus singling out modern readers, such statements imply that the ancient audience of the Bible was exempt from the difficulties faced by modern readers. Further, the unstated but widely held implication is that if a modern translation is not couched "in a manner and form easily understood by the readers" (GNB preface), the fault lies with the translation. Indeed, one finally gets the impression from the dynamic equivalence camp that literal translations are guilty of *making* the Bible difficult.

Over against the claims of a naive modern audience that is in a special position in finding the Bible difficult, I incline to the view that there is much about the Bible that is inherently difficult and technical. Surely Anthony Nichols is correct when he writes, "One cannot escape the fact that the Bible contains many concepts and expressions which are difficult for the modern reader. There is no evidence that they were much less so for the original readers. They, too, had to cope with technical terminology, with thousands of OT allusions and with Hebrew loan words, idioms and translation that must have been very strange to many of them."[21]

[21] Anthony H. Nichols, "Translating the Bible: A Critical Analysis of E. A. Nida's Theory of Dynamic Equivalence and Its Impact Upon Recent Bible Translations," dissertation, University of Sheffield, 1996, 298.

In a similar vein, Wayne Grudem pictures the situation thus: "Lest we think that understanding the Bible was somehow easier for first-century Christians than for us, it is important to realize that in many instances the New Testament epistles were written to churches that had large proportions of Gentile Christians. They were relatively new Christians who had no previous background in any kind of Christian society, and who had little or no prior understanding of the history and culture of Israel. The events of Abraham's life . . . were as far in the past for them as the events of the New Testament are for us!"[22]

In connection with preserving the difficulty of the original text, let us note a paradox in regard to the criterion of transparency that regularly enters contemporary discussion of translation principles. Essentially literal translators aim to make their translation *transparent to the original text*. This means preserving as much as possible of what the original authors wrote, including the difficulties and unfamiliar features of the original text. Dynamic equivalence translations aim to be transparent to the modern reader. Essentially literal translations do not *make* the Bible obscure and difficult but instead pass on the original text as it is. Sometimes it is difficult and obscure, but let me reiterate my claim that *all* modern translations are readable to educated people, including children.

REVERSING THE MYTHS ABOUT ESSENTIALLY LITERAL BIBLE TRANSLATION

I will summarize my five main points by stating them in a format that corrects the misconceptions that detractors of essentially literal translation have asserted.

1. When essentially literal translators respect and preserve the words of the original, they are not engaging in idolatry but are instead practicing what the Bible itself says about the primacy of words in God's revelation of his truth in Scripture.

2. There are two ways in which essentially literal translations are simple or naive, namely, in being uninterested in complex linguistic theory and in sticking with translation rather than mingling commentary

---

[22] Wayne Grudem, *Bible Doctrine: Essential Teachings of the Christian Faith* (Grand Rapids, Mich.: Zondervan, 1999), 55.

and editorializing with the translation. Dynamic translation is naive in more ways than this.

3. Essentially literal translations are genuine translations, not transcriptions or transliterations.

4. Essentially literal translations make a necessary distinction between linguistic or lexical interpretation and other types of interpretation, and refuse to add the activities of the exegete and the editor to the task of the translator.

5. Essentially literal translations are fully readable, and where their renderings are difficult or do not carry all of the meaning on the surface, they are being true to the original text.

Essentially literal translation theory and practice are regularly misrepresented by devotees of dynamic equivalence. I have attempted to correct what must be frankly acknowledged often to be caricatures. However, the current debate is more than an intellectual inquiry into correct translation principles and a dispelling of erroneous claims about essentially literal Bible translations. What is at stake is whether the Bible reading public will return to the real Bible or accept a substitute for it.

3

WHAT THE READER WANTS AND THE TRANSLATOR CAN GIVE:

First John as a Test Case

C. JOHN COLLINS

INTRODUCTION

Several English Bible translations have appeared in the last ten years, including the Contemporary English Version (CEV) in 1995, the New Living Translation (NLT) in 1996, the English Standard Version (ESV) in 2001, Today's New International Version (TNIV: New Testament, 2001; complete Bible, 2005), and the Holman Christian Standard Bible (HCSB) in 2004. The translation philosophies behind these versions differ in important ways, and these differences have precipitated vigorous discussion. Of course a "hot topic" has been the approach to translating gender language; but the perceptive have seen that this question is closely tied to the wider question of what constitutes translation.

I called the discussion "vigorous," and that is what it *should* be. The issues reach far beyond the linguistic and theological academy, right to the kind of Bible ordinary people will read, study, and use in church. When we add to that the sense of desperation at the decreasing Bible literacy of English-speaking culture, and the seemingly enormous task of reaching our fellows, we can see that too much is at stake to leave the matter solely in the hands of the specialists. On the other hand, we need the specialist for his or her advanced insight into the problems. But even here we have trouble: the specialists do not all say the same things.

While the discussions have been vigorous, I am not sure that they have always been productive; it seems at times that the various sides talk past each other, and even focus on caricatures of their opponents in order to win an easy victory. I think that much of this misunderstanding comes from the differing assumptions and definitions that each party brings to the discussion (and possibly some of these are not even explicit). As Greenstein put it,

> I can get somewhere when I challenge the deductions you make from your fundamental assumptions. But I can get nowhere if I think I am challenging your deductions when in fact I am differing from your assumptions, your presuppositions, your premises, your beliefs.[1]

Further, it is easy to score points against an opponent by selecting out particular Bible passages, and this is what many reviews have done: but this fails, whether because the translation under review may or may not reflect its stated philosophy well in that particular place, or because the reviewer may or may not understand how the translators applied their philosophy, or because we have to see how the version performs on a whole body of text.

In view of this, here is what I aim to do: first, I will consider what an ordinary person might think of as "translation"; second, I will aim to make this more rigorous by considering the dynamics of communication;[2] third, I will compare how the various approaches to translation perform on a continuous text, namely 1 John.

ORDINARY NOTIONS OF TRANSLATION

A. J. Krailsheimer was a teacher of French at Oxford, and translated a few French works into English. He was certainly, therefore, familiar with the task of translation, without himself being a theorist of the endeavor. Here is how he explained his goal in translating Pascal's *Pensées*:

---

[1] E. L. Greenstein, "The Role of Theory in Biblical Criticism," *Proceedings of the Ninth World Congress of Jewish Studies: Jerusalem, August 4-12, 1985* (Jerusalem: World Union of Jewish Studies, 1986), 167-174, at 167.

[2] Compare my approach in *Science and Faith: Friends or Foes?* (Wheaton, Ill.: Crossway, 2003), chapter 2: we make a mistake if we let the philosophers or scientists define what rationality is for us. "A good philosophy will start from everyday rationality and build on it, and refine it" (21).

The purpose of any translation is to enable those who have little or no knowledge of the original language to read with reasonable confidence works which would otherwise have been inaccessible to them. It does not help if the translator introduces variants of his own, instead of following as faithfully as possible the chosen original, ultimate criterion of accuracy and authenticity.[3]

Krailsheimer mentions one specific way in which he aimed at a "faithful" translation, which will be pertinent to our discussion below:

As regards the actual translation I have tried to follow one cardinal principle apparently rejected by most previous translators of Pascal: I know of no other author who repeats the same word with such almost obsessive frequency as Pascal, and failure to render this essential feature of his style makes a translation not only inadequate but positively misleading. Wherever possible, and especially within the same fragment or section, I have used one English word for the same keyword recurring in French.[4]

(Krailsheimer acknowledges that "some keywords . . . cannot be treated with absolute consistency.")

That Krailsheimer's goal is what the ordinary person thinks of as translation becomes clear if we consider something where we have no emotional investment. I teach Latin to my children, so my sister gave me a Latin *Daily Phrase and Culture Calendar* for 2000.[5] In this calendar, most days have a Latin phrase and a suggested translation, and sometimes a "literal" translation in brackets. Consider the entry for May 10:

Mutatis mutandis.
After making the necessary changes.
(lit.: Things having been changed that had to be changed.)

---

[3] A. J. Krailsheimer, in Blaise Pascal, *Pensées*, A. J. Krailsheimer, trans. and ed. (London: Penguin, 1995 [1670]), xxviii.
[4] Krailsheimer in ibid., xxix; and Krailsheimer appeals to Pascal's own principle in *Pensée* 515: "When words are repeated in an argument and one finds, on trying to correct them, that they are so apposite that it would spoil the work to change them, they must be left in."
[5] Published by the Living Language division of Random House.

The "literal" version offered is a fairly straight rendering of the Latin, even following the word order, but does not sound very good in English. We could rework it as *the things that had to be changed having been changed,* and from there to *the necessary changes having been changed;* here we see that the repetition of *change* is the offender. So we would end up with *the necessary changes having been made,* and we can see that the proffered translation simply gives us the active version of that. We would have no difficulty in calling *the necessary changes having been changed* a "literal but rough" translation, and *the necessary changes having been made* a "smoothed literal" translation (or "essentially literal" or "transparent," as we shall see below).

Consider what we get for July 1:

Ubi leges valent, ibi populus potest valere. (Publilius Syrus)
Where the laws are good, there the people are flourishing.

This translation might be "literal" after a fashion, but it is a failure, because it does not capture the repetition of *valere.*[6] It would be better to render, *where the laws are healthy, there the people can be healthy.* This shows that a mere word-for-word translation does not fulfill Krailsheimer's aim; it must also let you see something of the literary effect of the original.

Here is one that works reasonably well (April 16):

Quod cibus est aliis, aliis est venenum.
One man's meat is another man's poison.
(lit.: That which is food to some is poison to others.)

Actually, the "literal" version here is not quite literal enough, since it does not capture the chiasmus: *What is food to some, to others is poison.* The proffered translation aims to convey the aphoristic quality of the Latin by giving us an English proverb of virtually identical import.[7] We might call this translation an "almost literal" one.

---

[6] It also leaves out the potential *potest,* "can."

[7] The proverb has archaic features that might mislead some contemporary readers, however. I assume that the word "meat" is used in its older sense of "food"; and nowadays one must be careful about using "man" for "human person."

But aphoristic sayings are asking for trouble, as my two final examples show. For August 27 we get:

Pares cum paribus facillime congregantur. (Cicero)
Birds of a feather flock together.
(lit.: Equals most easily congregate with equals.)

The sense of the Latin words have exercised virtually no control over that of the English (unless we count *flock* and *congregate* as being semantic kin). But when we turn to June 20, we find something that is off the charts:

Mundus vult decipi.
There's a sucker born every minute.
(lit.: The world wants to be deceived.)

Few lay people would call these last two "accurate" translations, because the words of the original have exercised no control over the renderings.

TRANSLATION AND THE COMMUNICATION SITUATION

It is common to find translations put on a continuum between two poles, the "literal" and the "idiomatic," or the "formal equivalent" and the "dynamic [or functional] equivalent." Usually you can tell where a person's sympathies lie by the way he describes the two. For example, consider:

> There are two general theories or methods of Bible translation. The first has been called "formal equivalence." According to this theory, the translator attempts to render each word of the original language into the receptor language and seeks to preserve the original word order and sentence structure as much as possible. The second has been called "dynamic equivalence" or "functional equivalence." The goal of this translation theory is to produce in the receptor language the closest natural equivalent of the message expressed by the original-language text—both in meaning and in style. Such a translation attempts to have the same impact on modern readers as the original had on its own audience.

This comes from the introduction to the NLT, which is a dynamic equivalence version.[8]

Although the NLT presents formal versus dynamic equivalence as an antithesis, most recognize it as a continuum:[9]

literal	dynamic

Under this scheme, the publicity for the NIV and TNIV can represent that translation as having found the sweet spot between the poles, calling itself a "balanced, mediating version—one that would fall about halfway between the most literal and the most free."[10] Thus we might rank Bible versions along the scale:[11]

literal					dynamic		
RV NASB	KJV	RSV/ESV	NIV		NLT	TEV	CEV

I have argued elsewhere that this model is inadequate,[12] because it does not allow for what might be called an "essentially literal" or "transparent" translation, as R. C. Van Leeuwen describes it:

> A transparent translation conveys as much as possible of what was said, and how it was said, in as near word-for-word form as the target language allows, though inevitably with some difference and imperfectly.[13]

[8] The introduction goes on to say, "A thought-for-thought translation prepared by a group of capable scholars has the potential to represent the intended meaning of the original text even more accurately than a word-for-word translation."

[9] For example, Eugene A. Nida, *Toward a Science of Translating: With Special Reference to Principles Involved in Bible Translating* (Leiden: Brill, 1964), 24; J. Beekman and J. Callow, *Translating the Word of God* (Grand Rapids, Mich.: Zondervan, 1974), 21.

[10] K. L. Barker, "The Balanced Translation Philosophy of the TNIV," *Light Magazine, Special Edition: Shedding Light on the TNIV* (International Bible Society, 2002), 18-21, at 19.

[11] This is similar to the diagram found in Barker, "Balanced Translation Philosophy of the TNIV," 21. The main difference is that Barker (or the artist) has put the KJV in the "most literal" category, and this is contrary to, e.g., Nida, *Translating,* 17. (See discussion below.)

[12] C. John Collins, "Without Form You Lose Meaning," pages 295-327 in Leland Ryken, *The Word of God in English: Criteria for Excellence in Bible Translation* (Wheaton, Ill.: Crossway, 2002), at 296-298.

[13] R. C. Van Leeuwen, "We Really Do Need Another Bible Translation," *Christianity Today,* October 22, 2001, 28-35, at 30. See also Van Leeuwen, "On Bible Translation and Hermeneutics," in C. Bartholomew et al., eds., *After Pentecost: Language and Biblical Interpretation* (Grand Rapids, Mich.: Zondervan, 2001), 284-311.

This translation philosophy has been misunderstood, so I must amplify it a little more. The goal is for the syntax and semantics of the original text to govern the translation in such a way that such things as text genre, style (including irony and word-play), and register,[14] figurative language, interpretive ambiguities, and important repetitions show through.

Let me use an example: everyone knows that pure transcription is not translation, because the syntax and lexicon of one language do not line up uniformly with those of another. Hence the final phrase of the Tenth Commandment (Ex. 20:17), in a transcription, would be "and all which to-neighbor-of-you": this is not English, so it is not any kind of translation. A woodenly "literal" rendering would be, "and all which *is* to your neighbor" (this seems to be what the NLT preface means by "formal equivalence"). A transparent rendering, however (represented by ESV=RSV, compare KJV), would be, "or anything that is your neighbor's." This employs recognized linguistic operations to make smooth English: the sense "any" is part of the range of the Hebrew *kol* ("all"), translating a Hebrew verbless clause requires an English verb of being, and the datival preposition ("to") includes possession as part of its range (though this need not imply *ownership*).

In other words, the transparent (or essentially literal) translation philosophy agrees with everyone else that translation really does involve transferring a text from one language to another, but it aims to keep its interpretation to the level of recognized linguistic operations on the text. As this example shows, however, there is an interpretive ambiguity: since this clause finishes a list that includes a man's wife, does this imply that an Israelite man was seen as *owning* his wife? The Hebrew does not of itself answer the question: to give an answer would take a study of the law as a whole.[15] Other translations have not left the ambiguity intact: "or anything that *belongs to* your neighbor" (NIV); "or anything else your neighbor *owns*" (NLT, compare TEV, CEV). These imply the interpretation that the man does

---

[14] For a jarring mismatch in register, compare the solemn "woe to you" with the sputtering "damn you" in the Jesus Seminar's *Five Gospels*.
[15] For such a study, showing that the man does not own his wife, see Christopher Wright, *God's People in God's Land* (Carlisle, UK: Paternoster, 1997), 181-221, on the wife's status in Old Testament law.

indeed own his wife, and make it difficult for the English reader to consider another option.[16]

This means that the single-line continuum does not give enough insight into the translation situation; a better diagram might be:

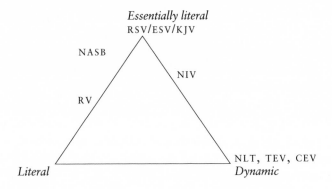

(I will justify later, as needed, the places I have assigned to the versions.)

This is an improvement, but it still does not capture the complexity of translation. Consider what place a text has in an act of communication. It is far too simple to say that we have a speaker, an audience, and a message that connects them. Rather, we should see that the speaker and audience have a picture of the world that to some extent they share between them: that picture includes, for example, knowledge, beliefs, values, experiences, language, and rhetorical conventions. For example, I am writing this essay in English, and I assume that you know what I mean by "the Hebrew Bible." A *text* is a means by which the speaker (or *author*) operates on that shared picture of the world to produce some effect (the *message*) in the audience: perhaps by adding new things for them to know, or by correcting things that they thought they knew; or by drawing on some part of it (such as their experience of God's love) in order for them to act upon it; or by evoking some aspect of it for celebration or mourning; or even by radically revising their orientation to

---

[16] When people refer to a translation as "interpretive," they are not usually denying that some degree of interpretation goes on at the linguistic level; they are instead saying that the interpretation has gone beyond what the linguistic details require, and that it forecloses interpretive options for the English reader. Those who defend dynamic equivalence do not often notice the distinction; perhaps a cumbersome phrase like "more interpretive than linguistically necessary" helps to convey the actual critique.

the world (their worldview). The authors and their audiences also share linguistic and literary conventions, which indicate how to interpret the text; for example, everyone who is competent in American English knows what to expect when a narrative begins with "once upon a time." For an audience to interpret a text properly, they must *cooperate* with the author as he has expressed himself in his text. (In terms used by the linguists, the "message" includes such things as illocutionary force, implicatures, and so on.)

The diagram would look like this:

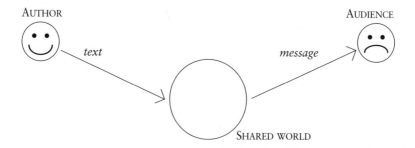

AUTHOR

text

AUDIENCE

message

SHARED WORLD

Since we are discussing Bible translating here, we must of course add another aspect, namely that of *appropriation* or *application:* by this we designate those in following times who read the text as part of their Bibles. The world of these later readers overlaps with that of the original communication, though only partially. This is actually a challenge for a translation that aims to be interdenominational, since there are no agreed-upon principles by which to appropriate the text.

This diagram allows us to bring some of the translation issues into focus: to what degree is translation based on the text alone, and to what degree should the translator supply information from the shared world, and how explicit should he make the "message." Before we look at Bible translation, let us consider some examples from other kinds of text.

My first example is William Blake's poem, "A poison tree":[17]

---

[17] Text in J. M. and M. J. Cohen, *The New Penguin Dictionary of Quotations* (Harmondsworth, UK: Penguin, 1992), 62:2.

I was angry with my friend:
I told my wrath, my wrath did end.
I was angry with my foe:
I told it not, my wrath did grow.

No doubt the poem uses a past incident to illustrate what always happens; in other words, the poem is equivalent in force to the poem with present tenses:

If I am angry with my friend,
I tell my wrath, my wrath does end.
If I am angry with my foe,
I tell it not, my wrath does grow.

But of course we should not stop there: the poet wants also to affect our behavior—that is his "message." Hence the poem is *pragmatically* equivalent to a translation with imperatives, purpose clauses, and second person reference:

When you're angry with your friend,
tell your wrath, that your wrath may end.
If you're angry with your foe,
don't tell it not, lest your wrath do grow.

Although these are *pragmatically* equivalent, they are not *rhetorically* equivalent: Blake's poem makes its impact precisely because of its concreteness (found in the past tenses), and its indirection (it leaves you to draw the conclusion).

Should a translation make the pragmatic force explicit? Not if the purpose of the translation is to allow the reader to listen in on the *English* poem.[18]

My second example is from C. S. Lewis's *Voyage of the Dawn Treader*.[19] In the first chapter, the return of the Pevensie children to

---

[18] There may, however, be occasions in which changing the tense from the past to the present may be necessary, if it is too difficult in the target language to infer from a specific event the normal pattern. This is the problem faced with the so-called gnomic tenses (in both Hebrew and Greek); on which see the discussion in C. John Collins, "Psalm 1: Structure and Rhetoric," *Presbyterion* 31 (2005): 37-48, appendix 2.

[19] C. S. Lewis, *The Voyage of the Dawn Treader* (New York: Macmillan, 1952).

Narnia for their second visit (recounted in *Prince Caspian*) is likened to King Arthur coming back to Britain. The translation into Modern Hebrew transposes this to King David coming back to the land of Israel.[20] This replaces something in the shared world of Lewis's audience with something in the world of the translator's audience, presumably for equivalent effect: but the result does not take the reader on a trip to *England*. A further move of this translator is to render the word "Lamb" (in the final chapter) with the Hebrew *taleh* rather than *seh*:[21] Lewis surely meant us to see here a reference to Christ, the sacrificed lamb, and the Hebrew New Testaments use *seh* for that. The Hebrew translation does not allow the reader even to consider the reference. I do not know whether ideological factors played a part here; but in any case, the translator has not shown the reader Lewis's world.

Now we can move on to look at Bible translation in the light of this improved communication model.

For example, if we explain that the chaff of Psalm 1:4 is "worthless" (as does NLT), we are bringing in factors from the shared world; we can go even further if we replace the imagery found in Psalm 1:3-4, based on the climate and agriculture of Palestine, with something with which the translator's audience is more familiar.[22] Since the literary conventions, such as poetic parallelism, are part of the shared world, then any operation we perform on that is likewise an effort to explicate or alter the appearance of that world.[23]

Some translators have thought that they must guide the reader in drawing out implicatures and interpreting figures—in other words, they

---

[20] C. S. Lewis, *Hammassa' be-Dorek Hashshachar*, Gideon Turi, trans. (Tel Aviv: Zmora, Bitan, Modan, 1979), 15.

[21] Lewis, *Hammassa' be-Dorek Hashshachar*, 178.

[22] For such a suggestion, see Robert Bratcher and William Reyburn, *A Translator's Handbook on the Book of Psalms* (New York: United Bible Societies, 1991), 19-20.

[23] For advice about how to handle Old Testament poetry, see Jan de Waard and William A. Smalley, *A Translator's Handbook on the Book of Amos* (London: United Bible Societies, 1979), page 11: "However, the important point to remember here is that such parallelism should come into a translation where it contributes to effective communication in the language of the translation and should not be carried over only because it is in the Hebrew or an English translation of the Hebrew. This means that quite often when something is said twice in the Hebrew in this way, it will be said only once in good translation." See further Ernst Wendland, *Comparative Discourse Analysis and the Translation of Psalm 22 in Chichewa, a Bantu Language of South-Central Africa* (Lewiston, N.Y.: Edwin Mellen, 1993) for the suggestion that we must seek an "equivalent" genre in the target language as well. It is often said that the translation strategy behind parts of the LXX (such as Proverbs) adapts the Biblical world to that of Alexandria, even extending to the world*view*.

go beyond the linguistic requirements of the *text* in order to convey the
message. Consider, for example, three versions of Proverbs 5:15-19:

ESV	NLT	TEV
[15]Drink water from your own cistern, flowing water from your own well.	Drink water from your own well—share your love only with your wife.	Be faithful to your own wife and give your love to her alone.
[16]Should your springs be scattered abroad, streams of water in the streets?	Why spill the water of your springs in public, having sex with just anyone?	Children that you have by other women will do you no good.
[17]Let them be for yourself alone, and not for strangers with you.	You should reserve it for yourself. Don't share it with strangers.	Your children should grow up to help you, not strangers.
[18]Let your fountain be blessed, and rejoice in the wife of your youth,	Let your wife be a fountain of blessing for you. Rejoice in the wife of your youth.	So be happy with your wife and find your joy with the girl you married—
[19]a lovely deer, a graceful doe. Let her breasts fill you at all times with delight; be intoxicated always in her love.	She is a loving doe, a graceful deer. Let her breasts satisfy you always. May you always be captivated by her love.	pretty and graceful as a deer. Let her charms keep you happy; let her surround you with her love.

The fully dynamic versions, NLT and TEV, have abandoned the poetic format of the Hebrew, and printed their material as prose paragraphs. They
have also aimed to spell out what they see as the implied behavioral force
of the text—though they differ on the consequences of unfaithfulness:
the NLT sees it as focused on the husband and wife relationship, while
the TEV sees it as including children (both illegitimate and one's own).[24]
As a matter of fact, I think they are both wrong: surely verses 16-17 push
a man to ask himself the question, "How would I feel if my wife were
promiscuous?"—in order to foster his commitment to avoiding adultery
on his own part.[25]

It has become conventional in translation literature to separate *form*
from *meaning,* with the implication that it is *meaning* that translation
conveys. Although there is a sense in which this is obvious—see the discussion of Exodus 20:17 above—the statement as it is normally made

---

[24] We might add as well the TEV's more delicate (or prudish) "charms" for "breasts."
[25] In verse 15, the wife is the water source, and verse 16 portrays this source as fouled by multiple users.

leads to some difficulties. To begin with, just what is the meaning of *meaning?* Is it a feature of the syntax (including discourse, paragraph, and sentence levels) and lexical sense of the text, or does it include the referential world (and if so, how much?), or does it even extend to the pragmatics? This is, of course, a well-known problem; but it is rarely spelled out—a situation that leads easily to equivocation on terms. Another difficulty is similar, namely the fact that *form* might have more than one level as well. The *literary* form of Proverbs 5:15-19, with its poetry and imagery, requires that the reader exercise his imagination in order to cooperate. The dynamic versions have tended to emphasize the cognitive content—which itself implies a particular notion of what communication (and possibly even human wholeness) is.[26] Further, the effort to make the *message* explicit interposes the translator between the text and the reader, and, as we can see in the case of Proverbs 5:16-17, translators do not always agree.

Another matter, into which I do not intend to delve, is that of gender language. For example, the address of Proverbs 6:1, "my son," is certainly to a male child—that is the sense of the Hebrew. It is part of the literary convention of Hebrew wisdom to be concrete, allowing the reader to apply it, *mutatis mutandis.* Consider, however, how the NLT translation handles this:[27]

> The Hebrew term *my son* (or *my sons*) is used twenty-seven times in the book of Proverbs. In most instances, as in this verse, the message applies equally to sons or daughters, so the NLT translates it "my child." Note, however, that the literal translation is retained in 5:1, 7, since the message of that entire chapter is clearly addressed to young men.

This conflates matters of sense (in the text) and reference (in the shared world) with what may—or may not—be the legitimate range of application.[28]

---

[26] Compare the distinction between "digital" and "analogical" language in Paul Fueter, "The Therapeutic Language of the Bible," *International Review of Mission* 75 (July 1986): 211-221 = *The Bible Translator* 37, no. 3 (1986): 309-319.

[27] *Holy Bible: New Living Translation,* Text and Product Preview (Wheaton, Ill.: Tyndale, 1996), 18.

[28] Because this goes beyond the sense and syntax of the words, this would be another example of a translation that is "more interpretive than linguistically necessary."

Everyone acknowledges that differences of judgment concerning the approach to translation will depend on the purpose for which the translation is to be used; but there is something even deeper, namely the very definition of "translation." Consider how Nida defines translation:

> To translate is to try to stimulate in the new reader in the new language the same reaction to the text as the one the original author wished to stimulate in his first and immediate readers.[29]

If we *define* translation this way, then of course we must embrace the functional equivalence approach; we must even include the part I have called the *message* in our rendering. But if we think of translation the way that Krailsheimer did in rendering Pascal, we might define translation more generally as something like, "allowing the reader to listen in on the foreign language communication." Then we can go on to speak of different kinds of "listening in."

This allows us to address the question of whether a translation should "sound like" a translation. The difficulty with this is in being clear on what we might mean. On the one hand, as we saw in the Exodus 20:17 example, we want the product to be grammatical and intelligible in the target language. On the other hand, the shared world between the author and his audience is inherently *foreign:* whether it be in regard to the things they share knowledge about, or in regard to genres, or to rhetorical conventions, or to ideology. A translation whose goal is to allow us to listen in on the original act of communication ought to display some of the "local color" of that act. Some dynamic versions reduce idioms and even major metaphors (such as "walking" for one's moral conduct) to more prosaic renderings, and thus lose some of that local color.[30]

As Anthony Nichols put it,

---

[29] Eugene Nida, cited in Robert G. Bratcher, "The Nature and Purpose of the New Testament in Today's English Version," *The Bible Translator* 22, no. 3 (1971): 97-107, at 98. See also Eugene A. Nida and Charles R. Taber, *The Theory and Practice of Translation* (Leiden: Brill, 1982), 1: "The new focus [in translating], however, has shifted from the form of the message to the response of the receptor"; on page 28 they use the receptors' response as a criterion of accuracy.

[30] Indeed, when the BBC reported that scientists think the universe is shaped like a "football," I had to remember what a British football is; and when a Briton refers to something as an "own goal" or "queering the pitch," I need to know something about soccer. But if a translator reduces these idioms, he also reduces the feel of traveling to Britain.

A translation of the Bible, in principle, should aim to retain as far as possible the exegetical potential of the source text. This would mean in practice that a good translation of the NT will preserve a sense of historical and cultural distance. . . . It will take the modern reader back into the alien milieu of first century Judaism where the Christian movement began. It will show him how the gospel of Jesus appeared to a Jew, and not how that Jew would have thought had he been an Australian or an American.[31]

CONSIDERING DIFFERENT KINDS OF TRANSLATIONS

This leads us to consider what kind of Bible translation might be suited to a particular context. Nida and Taber argued for this, distinguishing the contexts by the social stratum of the intended audience:

> For languages with a long literary tradition and a well-established traditional text of the Bible, it is usually necessary to have three types of Scriptures: (1) a translation which will reflect the traditional usage and be used in the churches, largely for liturgical purposes (this may be called an "ecclesiastical translation"), (2) a translation in the present-day literary language, so as to communicate to the well-educated constituency, and (3) a translation in the "common" or "popular" language, which is known to and used by the common people, and which is at the same time acceptable as a standard for published materials.[32]

The criteria we might use to distinguish the different contexts are—or should be—controversial. I might have divided the pie differently, based on characteristic uses rather than audiences: (1) a Bible for church; (2) a Bible for family reading, which includes children, and personal study; and (3) a Bible for outreach to the uninitiated. But the point remains: these different contexts might be best served by different translation philosophies. What kind of translation might suit these various contexts for the English reader?

---

[31] Anthony Nichols, "Dynamic Equivalence Bible Translations," *Colloquium: The Australian and New Zealand Theological Review* 19 (1986): 43-53, at 53.

[32] Nida and Taber, *Theory and Practice of Translation,* 31; see also what Nida told David Neff in the interview, "Meaning-full Translations: The World's Most Influential Bible Translator, Eugene Nida, Is Weary of 'Word Worship,'" *Christianity Today,* September 16, 2002, 46-49, at 49, where the third category is for "particular constituencies—children, for example."

The King James Version (KJV) held the field for at least the first two categories—whichever way we slice the pie—for about three centuries; and when it was first issued, it also supplied the third category of translation. At present, it cannot supply *any* of these categories, because too much of it reflects obsolete English.[33] But it has certainly set the pace for what the English Bible should "sound like," and an ecclesiastical translation should respect that.

Can we say what else we would ask for from an ecclesiastical translation? I do not intend here to venture into any kind of liturgical theology, specifying norms for anyone else. You can find a wide range of worship styles in the English-speaking world, from formal and structured to informal and free-flowing.[34] However, I do not believe that we must have liturgical uniformity to be able to say what features the Bible version should have.

I will simply list a few important features that I imagine most people will agree with (given enough supporting argument).[35] To begin with, the Bible version should be *intelligible*: that is, its English should be grammatical and broadly current without being too local in either time or place.[36] Second, it should be *ecumenical*: that is, it should serve Anglicans, Baptists, Calvary Chapelites, Dispensationalists, and so on throughout the alphabet soup of Christian bodies. Indeed, how good it would be if Eastern Orthodox, Protestants, and Roman Catholics had a common Bible (at least for the books on whose canonicity and textual basis they agree)! How else can we express our unity with other churches?

Third, a church Bible should be *orally rhythmic:* it should sound good even after countless readings aloud. Christian people have the Bible read aloud, not simply in the text before the sermon but also in

---

[33] Nida uses the fact that "hallowed be thy name" is mostly unintelligible today as an argument for "meaningful" translations (cited in Neff, "Meaning-full Translations," 46), but this hardly supports the idea of dynamic or functional equivalence; it only argues for intelligibility, which most translation philosophies endorse.

[34] Even so, it is still possible to analyze the sociolinguistics of language in worship. An English Roman Catholic author, David Crystal, has provided a useful discussion that extends beyond that denomination's boundaries: "Liturgical Language in a Sociolinguistic Perspective," in David Jasper and R. C. D. Jasper, eds., *Language and the Worship of the Church* (New York: St Martin's Press, 1990), 120-146.

[35] Ryken, *The Word of God in English*, elaborates on these and other desirable features in chapters 13-17.

[36] Of course there are judgment calls involved regarding what is "current"; and we further must allow for the variety of language levels in the Bible.

unison readings and Bible songs. Fourth, this Bible should be *preachable:* it should allow the preacher to preach from the text without having to wrestle with or correct the translation. The translators must be careful that they not limit the preacher's options beyond linguistic necessity. Please note: I am not here insisting that all preaching must be expository, after the model of Chrysostom—rather, I am simply saying that an adequate translation will not get in the way of those who wish to preach in this way.

And finally, its English style should be *poetic and dignified* (where the original is), without being stuffy. This last feature does not depend on whether the particular worship service itself is dignified or casual; I have attended, for example, a very lively and contemporary Calvary Chapel that used the NASB for the sermon because of their commitment to expository preaching.

A translation that echoes the language use and essentially literal philosophy of the KJV best suits this context.

Now consider the other categories of audience or use, as mentioned above. I prefer to think of the other categories by way of characteristic use rather than audience, because I hold that the question of which criteria we should use is not strictly a linguistic or sociological one—in which case a specialist in sociolinguistics does not necessarily have the advantage in discussing this. That is, I cannot accept theologically that the well-educated and the popular audiences should use different Bibles. It was not so in ancient Israel, nor in the early Christian church; and to make it so today would be to institutionalize (or even to baptize) distinctions of class and race that the apostles declared to be of no account (Col. 3:11).[37]

The characteristic use of the second category of translation, then, would be Bible reading and study in the home. As long as the ecclesiastical translation is intelligible, I see no reason for the home version to be different from the one used in church, except for the sake of variety from time to time. One might object, however, that the higher level of the language in this version excludes children; but in my own experience I have not found this to be a viable objection. Children—mine, at least—live up to what is expected of them, and aim to expand their language capacity anyhow; I do not find them to be embarrassed to admit that they do

---

[37] Compare also 1 Corinthians 1:31, in the context of verses 26-29.

not understand something, and the exercise of explaining a passage to young children has done me good. I admit that this puts more weight on parents' shoulders, but then our churches ought to welcome this, and equip their families for the task.

The third category of translation is the one for outreach. Here we might indeed prefer a Bible version simpler than the ecclesiastical one; but if we do use such a version, we should explain to people that its purpose is to be introductory. We need not apologize for the discipleship of the mind that Christian faithfulness calls us to; as C. S. Lewis observed in a work addressed to those outside the faith,

> [Christ] wants a child's heart, but a grown-up's head. He wants us to be simple, single-minded, affectionate, and teachable, as good children are; but He also wants every bit of intelligence we have to be alert at its job, and in first-class fighting trim. . . . If you are thinking of becoming a Christian, I warn you that you are embarking on something which is going to take the whole of you, brains and all.[38]

THE GREEK OF 1 JOHN

Let us see how different translation philosophies perform on a body of text, namely 1 John. Then we can say what philosophy is best suited to the various characteristic uses we discussed above.

I was sitting in church one day in the Spring of 2004, listening to a sermon series on 1 John, where the sermon text was the NIV (I had a Greek New Testament on one knee, and my son on the other). It struck me that this translation made it hard for the English reader to see the key features of the Greek text, and hard for the preacher to draw attention to these features.

As I sat, I drew up a list of those features that the translator ought to allow the English reader to see. Here is what I came up with (slightly revised after further reflection):[39]

---

[38] C. S. Lewis, *Mere Christianity* (New York: Scribner, 1952), book 3, chapter 2.

[39] Further on the features of the letter: Alfred Plummer, *The Epistles of St John: With Notes, Introduction and Appendices,* Cambridge Greek Testament for Schools and Colleges (Cambridge: Cambridge University Press, 1916), lvii-lxii; Brooke Foss Westcott, *The Epistles of St John: The Greek Text with Notes and Essays* (Cambridge: Macmillan, 1892), xxxix-xliii; Rudolph Schnackenburg, *The Johannine Epistles* (New York: Crossroad, 1992 [German 1984]), 6-11; Nigel Turner, *Style,* vol. 4 of *A Grammar of New Testament Greek* (Edinburgh: T & T Clark, 1976), 132-138; Ruth B. Edwards, *The Johannine Epistles,* New Testament Guides (Sheffield, UK: Sheffield Academic Press, 1996), 37-38.

1. The author repeats key terms throughout the book.
2. He uses generally simple vocabulary, syntax, and sentence conjunctions, to express profound thoughts (one reason why many Greek teachers use this book for beginning students).
3. Within this general simplicity there are some puzzling ambiguities (which is why I no longer use this book for beginners).
4. The author makes careful use of verbal aspect.
5. There are expressions of tender affection toward readers.
6. Even though there are no direct Old Testament citations, there are plenty of evocations.
7. There are important parallels with the Gospel of John.

I then made a table with parallel texts of the Greek and several English translations. I chose the ESV as a representative of the "transparent" strategy; the NLT as a "functional [or dynamic] equivalence" version, and the NIV as a "partly dynamic" version. I can justify these classifications from the translators' prefaces, but I will go further to show why the NIV is partly dynamic (since this may be controversial).

Robert Bratcher lists the basic tenets of the dynamic equivalence approach, based on its focus on equivalent response in the receptor: *contextual consistency over verbal consistency* ("no attempt is made to translate a given Greek word by the same word in English"), *naturalness* ("express the meaning of the original as naturally as possible in English"), *making implicit information explicit,* and *ready intelligibility* ("the meaning of idioms and figures of speech must be set forth plainly so that today's readers will understand them as did the readers of the original").[40] I will use these features in classifying the translations compared.

I have quoted the NLT preface already, noting its claim to be dynamic. The ESV preface claims,

> The ESV is an "essentially literal" translation that seeks as far as possible to capture the precise wording of the original text and the personal style of each Bible writer. As such, its emphasis is on "word-for-word" correspondence, at the same time taking into account differences of grammar, syntax, and idiom between current literary English and the original languages. Thus it seeks to be trans-

---

[40] Bratcher, "Nature and Purpose of the New Testament in Today's English Version," 98-100.

parent to the original text, letting the reader see as directly as possible the structure and meaning of the original.

The translators recognize that there are always trade-offs between "literal precision and readability," and thus they have not aimed to be woodenly literal. They further have set themselves deliberately in the KJV stream of language use, which gives the version a traditional feel. The NIV preface says,

> Because thought patterns and syntax differ from language to language, faithful communication of the meaning of the writers demands frequent modifications in sentence structure and constant regard for the contextual meanings of words.

There seem to be echoes of the form-meaning distinction here, as well as the priority of contextual consistency over verbal consistency, which are mainstays of dynamic equivalence theory. Our study of 1 John will verify that such considerations do in fact lie behind the NIV strategy, but not to the same extent as with the NLT.

Let us see how the different philosophies handle selected features of the Greek.[41] It might or might not be possible to convey all of these, but the degree to which we do determines how clear a window we provide into the original act of communication.

1. Repetition of Key Words

The author of 1 John repeats a number of words throughout his letter, such as μένω ("remain, abide"), especially in the combination μένω ἐν ("to abide in");[42] τηρέω ("to keep"), especially with objects such as "word" and "commands"; κόσμος ("world"); words related to ἀλήθεια ("truth"), ἀγάπη ("love"), ψεῦδος ("lie"). We might add some minor ones such as γεννάω ("to beget"); παρρησία ("confidence"); λέγω / εἶπον ("to say"); and τελειόω / τέλειος ("to perfect," "perfect").

The verb μένω ("abide") appears 24 times in 18 verses in 1 John

---

[41] In my private notes I have examined them all in detail, and these selections are intended to be representative.

[42] Compare as well ἐστίν ἐν ("to be in"). A book-length study of these terms is Edward Malatesta, *Interiority and Covenant,* Analecta Biblica (Rome: Biblical Institute Press, 1978).

(2:6, 10, 14, 17, 19, 24, 27, 28; 3:6, 9, 14, 15, 17, 24; 4:12, 13, 15, 16);
all but two of those (2:17, 19) use the combination μένω ἐν ("abide
in").[43] Believers *abide in* Christ, in the light, in the Son and in the Father,
and not in death; while God, or the word of God, or God's anointing,
or eternal life, or the love of God *abides in* the believer. These two kinds
of abiding—the believer's in God and God's in the believer—are two
sides of the same coin, alternate ways of describing genuine spiritual life.
A good illustration of the connection is 2:24 (compare also 2:27; 3:14-
15, 24; 4:16):

> Let what you heard from the beginning *abide in* you. If what you
> heard from the beginning *abides in* you, then you too will *abide in*
> the Son and in the Father (ESV).

This repetition is so prevalent that it must be part of the author's
intended literary effect.[44] The "essentially literal" tradition in English
(KJV, RSV, ESV) has successfully conveyed this repetition.[45]

How do the more dynamic versions perform? Consider first the fully
dynamic NLT. This version renders our verb with quite a variety of terms:
"live" (2:6, 10, 14, 17; 3:24b; 4:12, 13, 15, 16; *"continue to* live,"
2:27b; 3:6; "live *with,"* 2:27a);[46] "live in fellowship with" (3:24a; *"continue to* live in fellowship with," 2:24c, 28); "remain faithful" (2:24a);
"be" (3:9, 17; "be *still,"* 3:14); a dummy "do" (2:24b); and even no rendering at all (3:15). (The unusual 2:19 has "stay.") The explanation for
such variation seems to be the translators' adherence to the tenets of
dynamic equivalence, especially contextual consistency, naturalness,
and ready intelligibility.

Consider what happens in 2:24:

---

[43] Compare also John 5:38; 6:56; 8:31; 15:4, 5, 6, 7, 9, 10, 16.

[44] Recall Krailsheimer's remark on Pascal that we noted earlier: "I know of no other author who repeats
the same word with such almost obsessive frequency as Pascal, and failure to render this essential feature
of his style makes a translation not only inadequate but positively misleading." But now we can see that
1 John has equaled this obsession.

[45] In fact, the only occurrence of μένω that gets a different rendering in these versions is in 2:19, "they
would have *continued* with us." In defense of the tradition, we may note that this is not μένω ἐν.
Further, the past participle of English "abide" ("abode" or "abidden," or even "abided"?) has long been
problematic, as the OED testifies: the contrary-to-fact expression, "they would have abode/abidden
with us," sounds very awkward. Had the tradition used "remain," however, it could have captured even
this instance of the verb.

[46] Note that this version renders εἶναι ἐν "to be in" as "to live in" in 2:5; 4:4: perhaps the translators
decided that the "meaning" of the two is the same?

> So you must *remain faithful to* what you have been taught from the
> beginning. If you *do,* you will *continue to live in fellowship with* the
> Son and with the Father.

The connection that the Greek repetition establishes does not come
through at all.

The NIV renders our term with "live" (2:6, 10, 14, 17; 3:6, 24ab;
4:12, 13, 15, 16ab); "remain" (2:24ac, 27ab; 3:9, 14); "continue"
(2:28); "be" (3:17); a dummy "do" (2:24b), and no rendering at all
(3:15; 4:16c). (It uses "remain" in 2:19.) Although the variation is not
as much as we found in the NLT, it still appears that the NIV has also followed the principles of contextual consistency, naturalness, and ready
intelligibility.

Consider 2:24:

> See that what you have heard from the beginning *remains in* you. If
> it *does,* you also will *remain in* the Son and in the Father.

At least here the repetition comes through; but just a few verses later
(2:27-28) we find:

> (27) As for you, the anointing you received from him *remains in* you,
> and you do not need anyone to teach you. But as his anointing teaches
> you about all things and as that anointing is real, not counterfeit—
> just as it has taught you, *remain in* him. (28) And now, dear children,
> *continue in* him, so that when he appears we may be confident and
> unashamed before him at his coming.

This shows that displaying the repetition over a long stretch of the text
was not a goal for the NIV.

We might criticize the dynamic versions further by asking whether
"live" and "live in fellowship with" are semantically accurate, when the
Greek verb is used for the nuance of remaining or enduring. This would
certainly give difficulty to a reader or preacher who wanted to point out
the repetition and its implications. Indeed, one recent commentary on
1 John (which uses the NIV as its running English text), expounding 2:17
(NIV "lives forever"), cites passages from John's Gospel where "Jesus

stresses that those who believe in him . . . shall never perish but shall live and remain forever" (the passages are John 6:51, 58; 8:51; 10:28; 11:26), and none of them uses μένω.[47] I believe the commentator was seriously hampered by the NIV translation strategy.

We could pursue this kind of study for the other repeated words, but space does not permit that—though we shall return to τηρέω and τελειόω / τέλειος in later discussions.

2. *Puzzling Ambiguities*

Anyone who reads 1 John carefully will be fascinated by the ambiguities we find there—that is, by the expressions that have more than one possible grammatical analysis, and it is not immediately clear which one the author intended. The tenets of dynamic equivalence push the translator to decide between the options on behalf of the reader (except in those cases where the translator recognizes the literary effect of the ambiguity), since too much ambiguity is taken as a blemish.[48]

If, on the other hand, the Greek expressions themselves are ambiguous, it is quite possible that the extra effort it takes to decode them is part of the communicative act. It is also true that different expositors will analyze these differently; and a translation that resolves them ties the expositor's hands.[49]

One of these ambiguities in 1 John is the expression ἡ ἀγάπη τοῦ θεοῦ / τοῦ πατρός / αὐτοῦ "the love of God / of the Father / of him" (2:5, 15; 3:17; 4:9, 12; 5:3): is this "love *for* God," or "God's love," or "love that comes from God," or something else?[50]

We could argue that since the cognate verb ἀγαπάω appears in phrases of the type "believers love God" (4:20, 21; 5:1, 2), then the genitive is objective ("love *for* God"). However, phrases of the type "God

---

[47] Colin G. Kruse, *The Letters of John,* Pillar New Testament Commentary (Grand Rapids, Mich.: Eerdmans, 2000), 96-97.

[48] Compare Nida and Taber, *Theory and Practice of Translation,* 7-8.

[49] Compare Anthony Nichols, "Explicitness in Translation and the Westernization of Scripture," *Reformed Theological Review* 47, no. 3 (1988): 78-88.

[50] The same ambiguity exists in the English construction. We can see that such ambiguity is a property of *native* English (and not just translation) from the way John McKay answered a reporter's question. McKay was lured away from a successful career at USC to be the first coach of the Tampa Bay Buccaneers; and after the final loss in an 0-14 season, he was asked, "What do you think of the execution of your team?" McKay replied, "I'm all for it." (Cited from Ron Cook's column in the *Pittsburgh Post-Gazette,* February 28, 2004, accessed October 28, 2004, at http://www.post-gazette.com/pg/ 04039/270287.stm.)

loves people" also appear (4:11, 19), so we cannot rule out "God's love" or "love *from* God." (In 4:10 they appear together!) Westcott concluded that the expression describes "the love that God has made known," while Bruce concluded just the opposite: it is "our love for God."[51] I do not need to adjudicate at this point; it is enough to make the difficulty clear.

The essentially literal approach will be to pass the responsibility on to the reader to decide, just as the readers of the Greek had to decide. Hence the ESV renders these as "the love of God" (2:5; 4:9; 5:3) and "the love of the Father" (2:15). In two places the rendering probably steers away from the objective genitive: "God's love" (3:17) and "his love" (4:12)—although an expositor who wanted to do so could describe it as "the love that is due to God from us."

The dynamic NLT decides in favor of the objective genitive some times, "really do love [God]" (2:5), "loving God" (5:3); and the subjective genitive at others, "he loved us" (4:9). Though 4:12 in the NLT has "his love" like the ESV, the sentence "his love has been brought to full expression" leaves little room for anything other than the subjective genitive. In 2:15 and 3:17 the rendering is open like the ESV.

The NIV leaves the expression ambiguous in 2:15; 3:17, and, if we include "God's / his love," the ambiguity appears also in 2:5; 4:12. In 4:9 it is taken as a subjective genitive ("God showed his love"), while in 5:3 it is objective ("love for God").

Each of these versions has been true to its principles. Now, it may be that one should take all of these genitives the same way, or that we should find a mixture. Only the essentially literal approach consistently leaves the decision to the reader and expositor, however.

The ambiguous genitive appears in 2:5; 4:12, 17, 18, in a phrase that is itself ambiguous, involving the repetition of the verb τελειόω ("to make perfect or complete," 2:5; 4:12, 17, 18) and its cognate adjective τέλειος ("perfect or complete," 4:18). Consider 2:5 (Greek and ESV):

ἀληθῶς ἐν τούτῳ ἡ ἀγάπη τοῦ θεοῦ   in him truly the love of God is
τετελείωται   perfected

---

[51] Westcott, *Epistles of St John*, 48-49; F. F. Bruce, *The Epistles of John* (Grand Rapids, Mich.: Eerdmans, 1970), 51-52.

Does this mean that the person perfectly loves God,[52] or that God's saving love has reached its perfect goal—and if it has done so, how?[53] And how does this connect to "perfect love," and being "perfected in love" (4:18)?

To convey the force of the Greek, a translation should display the repetition, and allow the reader to puzzle it out. Consider how the three versions perform:

ESV	NIV	NLT
[2:5]but whoever keeps his word, in him truly *the love of God is perfected.*	But if anyone obeys his word, *God's love is* truly *made complete* in him.	But those who obey God's word *really do love him.*
[4:12]No one has ever seen God; if we love one another, God abides in us and *his love is perfected in us.*	No one has ever seen God; but if we love one another, God lives in us and *his love is made complete* in us.	No one has ever seen God. But if we love each other, God lives in us, and *his love has been brought to full expression through us.*
[4:17]By this *is love perfected with us,* so that we may have confidence for the day of judgment, because as he is so also are we in this world.	In this way, *love is made complete among us* so that we will have confidence on the day of judgment, because in this world we are like him.	And as we live in God, *our love grows more perfect.* So we will not be afraid on the day of judgment, but we can face him with confidence because we are like Christ here in this world.
[4:18]There is no fear in love, but *perfect love* casts out fear. For fear has to do with punishment, and whoever fears *has not been perfected in love.*	There is no fear in love. But *perfect love* drives out fear, because fear has to do with punishment. The one who fears *is not made perfect in love.*	Such love has no fear because *perfect love* expels all fear. If we are afraid, it is for fear of judgment, and this shows that *his love has not been perfected in us.*

As before, I have not set out to resolve the interpretive difficulties, only to evaluate how well the translation allows the English reader to see the issues and decide for himself. The ESV has shown both the repetition and the ambiguity in the kind of love. The NIV—which, as we saw above, tends to resolve the ambiguities—has almost shown the repetition with "made complete" (2:5, 4:12, 17), though it inexplicably veered off to "made perfect" in 4:18. The NLT, true to its dynamic principles, has no interest in this kind of repetition: instead it has sought "contextual consistency" and ready intelligibility.

---

[52] Compare, for example, Bruce, *Epistles of John,* 52; and Plummer, *Epistles of St John,* 38-39.
[53] Compare Malatesta, *Interiority and Covenant,* 128-132.

3. Old Testament Evocations

The usage of the Old Testament in 1 John is a fascinating study in its own right, and I will only be able to make a few observations here. The author does not cite an Old Testament text, and when he refers to one, as in 3:12 (Cain and Abel, Gen. 4:8), his key Greek term (σφάζω, "slay, murder") differs from that of the LXX (ἀποκτείνω, a less colorful term for "kill").[54]

On the other hand, there are plenty of evocations of the Old Testament, using the language of the LXX. For example, the notion of sacrificial blood "cleansing" or "purifying" from sin (1:7) comes from the Old Testament, as in Leviticus 16:19: "And he shall sprinkle some of the *blood* on it with his finger seven times, and *cleanse* (καθαρίζω, Hebrew *tihar*) it and consecrate it from the uncleannesses of the people of Israel" (compare also Heb. 9:14)—an evocation that all three versions allow their readers to see.

Similarly, the term ἱλασμός (2:2; 4:10) comes from sacrificial language: in Leviticus 25:9; Numbers 5:8 it represents Hebrew *kippurim*.[55] The Hebrew term is rendered as "atonement" in all three versions, while the Greek term in 1 John is "propitiation" (ESV), "atoning sacrifice" (NIV), and "sacrifice" (NLT). The NLT has under-translated, while the NIV has made the effort to show the connection with the Old Testament. The ESV is based on the conviction that the Greek term properly designates "propitiation," and follows that over the Old Testament connection.[56] Either the NIV or ESV can be justified as reasonable attempts to convey the Greek, whereas the NLT is due, apparently, more to the requirements of ready intelligibility.

Another important evocation of the Old Testament is the repeated use of τηρέω ("keep") with objects such as "word" and "commands" (2:3, 4, 5; 3:22, 24; 5:3).[57] The analogous expressions in Hebrew use the

---

[54] Interestingly enough, John's terms "evil" and "righteous" (πονηρός, δίκαιος) do not correspond to either the LXX or to anything in the MT: but the terms do resemble the near-contemporary Josephus, who (*Antiquities*, 1.53) said that Abel "had respect for *righteousness* (δικαιοσύνης ἐπεμελεῖτο), while Cain was "very *evil*" (πονηρότατος).

[55] For a brief discussion of New Testament uses of Old Testament sacrificial terminology to describe what Jesus accomplished in his dying, see C. John Collins, "The Eucharist as Christian Sacrifice," *Westminster Theological Journal* 66 (2004): 1-23, at 21-23.

[56] Compare the NIV margin, "the one who turns aside God's wrath"—which leaves out the notion of the *sacrifice* being the means of turning aside.

[57] Compare also John 8:51, 52, 55; 14:15, 21, 23, 24; 15:10, 20; 17:6.

verbs *shamar* and *natsar,*[58] both of which, when a command is the object, convey the notion of "keep, carefully attend to," and even "treasure."[59] The LXX renders these verbs mostly with φυλάσσω and τηρέω, with φυλάσσω predominating. In the New Testament both words are common, and appear to be interchangeable in such a context.

Apparently since the idea of "carefully attending to" God's commands implies obedience, the NIV and NLT have focused on that element for their translation: they have fastened on "obey" in most places, with "do" (2:4, NIV) and "keep" (5:3, NLT) appearing once each. This rendering does not allow the English reader to consider whether the term conveys more than obedience, extending into the *attitude* of the believer, and hence it does not allow him to ask the questions that a Greek reader would ask.

How do the more dynamic versions handle the relevant terms in the Old Testament? They vary, with the NIV being closer to the proper sense. (Of course, then, it is harder for the English reader to see how 1 John uses the Old Testament idea.) For example, in Psalm 105:45 we have "that they might *keep* (*shamar*) his statutes and *observe* (*natsar*) his laws" (ESV, NIV almost identical), but also "so they would *follow* his principles and *obey* his laws" (NLT). Consider a few verses from the first stanza of Psalm 119, a psalm that rings the changes on the attitude of delight in God's requirements:

ESV	NIV	NLT
[2]Blessed are those who *keep* his testimonies, who seek him with their whole heart.	Blessed are they who *keep* his statutes and seek him with all their heart.	Happy are those who *obey* his decrees and search for him with all their hearts.
[4]You have commanded your precepts to be *kept* diligently.	You have laid down precepts that are to be fully *obeyed*.	You have charged us to *keep* your commandments carefully.
[5]Oh that my ways may be steadfast in *keeping* your statutes!	Oh, that my ways were steadfast in *obeying* your decrees!	Oh, that my actions would consistently *reflect* your principles!
[8]I will *keep* your statutes; do not utterly forsake me!	I will *obey* your decrees; do not utterly forsake me.	I will *obey* your principles. Please don't give up on me!

[58] Delitzsch's Hebrew New Testament uses *shamar* in these places in 1 John, while the Syriac uses *netar* (the Aramaic cognate of Hebrew *natsar*).

[59] Compare Keith N. Schoville, "*shamar*," no. 9068 in W. A. VanGemeren, ed., *New International Dictionary of Old Testament Theology and Exegesis*, 5 vols. (Grand Rapids, Mich.: Zondervan, 1997), 4:182-184.

Again, the rendering "obey" is probably an under-translation.[60]

Consider the expression, "the last hour" (ἐσχάτη ὥρα), found twice in 2:18. Some have taken this to show that the author thought the end of the world was quite near (either in actuality, or at least potentially).[61] However, it seems far more likely to me that this term evokes the prophetic "last/latter days" of such texts as Isaiah 2:2 and Hosea 3:5 (Hebrew *be'acharit hayyamim;* ESV "in the latter days"; LXX ἐν ταῖς ἐσχάταις ἡμέραις / ἐπ᾽ ἐσχάτων τῶν ἡμερῶν [with other variations]).[62] In both Isaiah and Hosea the term denotes the times of the Messiah, and the New Testament uses it this way in Acts 2:17; 1 Peter 1:20; almost surely in Hebrews 1:2; James 5:3; and likely in 2 Timothy 3:1; 2 Peter 3:3; Jude 18.[63] This makes contextual sense of the "antichrist," a term unique to John's letters (1 John 2:18, 22; 4:3; 2 John 7). The antichrists oppose the Christ (or Messiah) by denying that Jesus is the Christ (come in the flesh).

As an expositor I will take one approach or another; but as a translator it is not my task to decide on behalf of the reader. The ESV and NIV allow the reader to see the term against its Old Testament background, while the NLT renders the term "the last hour" in its first appearance (the beginning of the verse), and "the end of the world" in its second (at the end of the same verse). When people refer to a translation as interpretive, this is just the sort of thing they have in mind: it shuts the English reader off from other options.

There are other possible Old Testament evocations,[64] but these will

---

[60] See also Proverbs 3:1b, where ESV has "let your heart *keep* my commandments." We cannot compare this with NIV and NLT, since they analyze the syntax differently (and wrongly, in my judgment): "keep my commands in your heart" (NIV) and "store my commands in your heart" (NLT). "Your heart" is surely the subject of the verb "keep" (*natsar*), as the ESV (see LXX and KJV) takes it, and this shows that attitude is in fact part of the meaning of the expression.

[61] For example, Plummer, *Epistles of St John,* 55-56; Bruce, *Epistles of John,* 64-65; C. Haas, M. de Jonge, and J. L. Swellengrebel. *A Translator's Handbook on the Letters of John,* Helps for Translators (London: United Bible Societies, 1972), 62; Kruse, *Letters of John,* 98.

[62] For ἐπ᾽ ἐσχάτων τῶν ἡμερῶν, see Gen. 49:1; Num. 24:14; Hos. 3:5; Mic. 4:1; Jer. 30:24; 49:39; Ezek. 38:16; Dan. 2:28. For ἐπ᾽ ἐσχάτῳ τῶν ἡμερῶν, see Deut. 4:30; 31:29; Dan. 10:14. For ἐν ταῖς ἐσχάταις ἡμέραις, see Isa. 2:2. For ἐπ᾽ ἐσχάτου τῶν ἡμερῶν, see Jer. 23:20. Ezek. 38:8 has "in the latter *years*" (LXX ἐπ᾽ ἐσχάτου ἐτῶν), which seems to be a variant of this term, as verse 16 shows (so Yechiel Moskovitz, *Sefer Yechezqel,* Da'at Miqra [Jerusalem: Mossad Harav Kook, 1985], 304n.8).

[63] See Westcott, *Epistles of St John,* 69. A similar interpretation, without appeal to the prophetic texts, appears in Theophylact, in J.-P. Migne, ed., *Patrologia Graeca,* 162 vols. (Turnhout, Belgium: Brepols), vol. 126, column 23.

[64] For example, consider 5:3, where God's commands are not βαρεῖαι (ESV/NIV "burdensome"); this rendering is far truer to the LXX usage of βαρύνω and βαρύς than the NLT "difficult" (compare Ex. 5:9; 1 Kings 12:4, 11, 14; Neh. 5:15, 18; Ps. 38:4; Isa. 47:6; Sir 40:1; 1 Macc. 8:31). Compare also the Syriac at 5:3, using *yaqqir* "heavy, oppressive."

suffice for the point. In the terms of my communication model above, these Old Testament patterns were part of the shared world between the author and his audience. A good translation is one that allows us to listen in on this communication—which means it allows the English reader to detect the evocations. Judged by this criterion, the essentially literal ESV outperforms the partly dynamic NIV, which outperforms the fully dynamic NLT. Again, this is not an accident: it is rather a case of the versions being true to their stated translation principles.

CONCLUSIONS

Let us survey where we have been, and what I think I have shown. First of all, we may dictate the translation philosophy by how we define "translation." Before we do that, though, we do well to stand back and consider what takes place in an act of communication. The model I have described above clarifies some of the challenges of translation: namely, to what extent we may properly explicate aspects of the shared world and the illocutionary force ("message"), and how much we should follow the sense and syntax of the text itself.

We cannot answer the simple question, which is the best approach to translation? We must instead qualify it: best for what purpose? I have argued that the essentially literal translation, carefully defined, is the kind of translation that best suits the requirements for an ecclesiastical translation, and for family reading and study. This is because it allows the reader to listen in on the original act of communication, but refrains from "clarifying" based on what we think we know of the shared world and the illocutionary force; it also aims to provide a translation that preserves the full exegetical potential of the original, especially as it conveys such things as text genre, style, and register, along with figurative language, interpretive ambiguities, and important repetitions. Of course this lays a heavier burden on the reader to learn about the shared world and its literary conventions, and we might decide not to lay this burden on the outsider to the Christian faith *in our outreach* (though we should make it clear that the burden exists).

In order to warrant this conclusion, I have examined some of the most obvious features of 1 John in the light of these considerations. Of the longer list I gave earlier, I selected three items: repetition of key terms;

puzzling ambiguities; and Old Testament evocations. I tested three translations in places where they were true to their stated translation philosophies: the ESV (essentially literal), the NIV (partly dynamic), and the NLT (dynamic equivalence). The essentially literal approach does the best job of allowing the English reader to see these features, and the fully dynamic equivalence approach does the worst. This means that if a careful preacher were to use a dynamic version, he would find himself arguing with the translation—and the more dynamic, the more the argument. A family reading 1 John in a dynamic version will be severely limited in its ability to see the ways that the author himself has signaled his communicative interests.

Although this study has been limited to some features of 1 John, it would not be hard to carry out a similar study, say, for Romans, or for Genesis 1–4, or Ecclesiastes, selected psalms, and so forth. My preliminary surveys of this material indicate that we will find the same conclusions.

What does the reader want, and what can the translator provide? An opportunity to listen in on the original foreign language communication, without prejudging what to do with that communication.

An irony arises from all this: the motive for the dynamic philosophy is a laudable one, namely to let everyone in on the wonders of the Bible, without allowing the experts to get in the way. Its result, however, is to interpose the translator between the reader and the text. The essentially literal philosophy, whose main interest is in doing justice to the original act of communication, opens up a new world to all manner of people, if they are willing to take the trouble to learn the customs of this foreign land.

BIBLIOGRAPHY

Barker, Kenneth L. "The Balanced Translation Philosophy of the TNIV." *Light Magazine,* 2002, 18-21.

Barnwell, Katharine. *Bible Translation: An Introductory Course in Translation Principles.* Dallas: Summer Institute of Linguistics, 1986.

Beekman, John, and John Callow. *Translating the Word of God.* Grand Rapids, Mich.: Zondervan, 1974.

Bratcher, Robert G. "The Nature and Purpose of the New Testament in Today's English Version." *The Bible Translator* 22, no. 3 (1971): 97-107.

Bratcher, Robert G., and William Reyburn. *A Translator's Handbook on the Book of Psalms.* New York: United Bible Societies, 1991.

Bruce, F. F. *The Epistles of John.* Grand Rapids, Mich.: Eerdmans, 1970.

Callow, Kathleen. *Discourse Considerations in Translating the Word of God.* Grand Rapids, Mich.: Zondervan, 1974.

Carson, D. A. "The Limits of Functional Equivalence in Bible Translation— and Other Limits, Too." Pages 65-113 in *The Challenge of Bible Translation.* Edited by Glen G. Scorgie, Mark L. Strauss, and Steven M. Voth. Grand Rapids, Mich.: Zondervan, 2003.

Chapple, Allan. "The English Standard Version: A Review Article." *Reformed Theological Review* 62, no. 2 (2003): 61-96.

Collins, C. John. "When Should We Translate *poieô* 'to Make' as 'to Reckon'?" *Selected Technical Articles Related to Translation,* no. 16 (1986): 12-32.

———. "Without Form, You Lose Meaning." Pages 295-327 in *The Word of God in English: Criteria for Excellence in Bible Translation.* Edited by Leland Ryken. Wheaton, Ill.: Crossway, 2002.

———. *Science and Faith: Friends or Foes?* Wheaton, Ill.: Crossway, 2003.

———. "The Eucharist as Christian Sacrifice." *Westminster Theological Journal* 66 (2004): 1-23.

———. "Psalm 1: Structure and Rhetoric." *Presbyterion* 31 (2005): 37-48.

Crisp, Simon. "Icon of the Ineffable? An Orthodox View of Language and Its Implications for Bible Translation." Pages 36-49 in *Bible Translation on the Threshold of the Twenty-first Century.* Edited by Athalya Brenner, and Jan Willem van Henten. London: Sheffield Academic Press, 2002.

Crystal, David. "Liturgical Language in a Sociolinguistic Perspective." Pages 120-146 in *Language and the Worship of the Church.* Edited by David Jasper, and R. C. D. Jasper. New York: St Martin's Press, 1990.

Davids, Peter H. "Three Recent Bible Translations: A New Testament Perspective." *Journal of the Evangelical Theological Society* 46, no. 3 (2003): 521-532.

de Regt, Lenart J. "Otherness and Equivalence in Bible Translation: A Response to Simon Crisp." Pages 50-52 in *Bible Translation on the Threshold of the Twenty-first Century.* Edited by Athalya Brenner, and Jan Willem van Henten. London: Sheffield Academic Press, 2002.

de Waard, Jan, and William A. Smalley. *A Translator's Handbook on the Book of Amos.* London: United Bible Societies, 1979.

Dryden, J. de Waal. "The Sense of *sperma* in 1 John 3:9." *Filologia Neotestamentaria* 9 (1998): 85-100.

Edwards, Ruth B. *The Johannine Epistles. New Testament Guides.* London: Sheffield Academic Press, 1996.

Eldridge, Michael D. "A New Addition to the King James Family." *Expository Times* 114, no. 7 (2003): 241-244.

Ellis, E. Earle. "Dynamic Equivalence Theory, Feminist Ideology and Three Recent Bible Translations." *Expository Times:* 1-5.

Fehderau, Harold W. "The Role of Bases and Models in Bible Translations." *The Bible Translator* 30 (1979): 401-414.

Fueter, Paul D. "The Therapeutic Language of the Bible." *International Review of Mission* 75 (1986): 211-221.

Funk, Robert, and Roy Hoover. *The Five Gospels.* New York: Macmillan, 1993.

Greenstein, E. L. "The Role of Theory in Biblical Criticism." Pages 167-74 in *Proceedings of the Ninth World Congress of Jewish Studies:* Jerusalem, August 4-12, 1985. Jerusalem: World Union of Jewish Studies, 1986.

Griffith, Terry. "A Non-Polemical Reading of 1 John: Sin, Christology and the Limits of Johannine Christianity." *Tyndale Bulletin* 49, no. 2 (1998): 253-276.

Gutt, Ernst-August. "What Is the Meaning We Translate?" *Occasional Papers in Translation and Textlinguistics* 1 (1987): 31-58.

Haas, C., M. de Jonge, and J. L. Swellengrebel. *A Translator's Handbook on the Letters of John.* Helps for Translators. London: United Bible Societies, 1972.

Hansford, Keir L. "The Underlying Poetic Structure of 1 John." *Journal of Translation and Textlinguistics* 5, no. 2 (1992): 126-174.

Jacobs, Alan. "A Bible for Everyone." *First Things,* no. 138 (2003): 10-14.

Kruse, Colin G. *The Letters of John.* Pillar New Testament Commentary. Grand Rapids, Mich.: Eerdmans, 2000.

Larson, Mildred L. *Meaning-Based Translation: A Guide to Cross-Language Equivalence.* Lanham: University Press of America, 1984.

Lewis, C. S. *The Voyage of the Dawn Treader.* New York: Macmillan, 1952.

———. *Mere Christianity.* New York: Scribner, 1952.

———. *Hammassa' be-Dorek Hashshachar.* Translated by Gideon Turi. Tel Aviv: Zmora, Bitan, Modan, 1979.

Lyons, John. *Language, Meaning and Context.* London: Fontana, 1981.

Lyons, Michael, and William A. Tooman. "Three Recent Bible Translations: An Old Testament Perspective." *Journal of the Evangelical Theological Society* 46, no. 3 (2003): 497-520.

Malatesta, Edward. *Interiority and Covenant*. Analecta Biblica. Rome: Biblical Institute Press, 1978.

Moskovitz, Yechiel. *Sefer Yechezqel*. Da'at Miqra. Jerusalem: Mossad Harav Kook, 1985.

Neff, David. "Meaning-Full Translations: The World's Most Influential Bible Translator, Eugene Nida, Is Weary of 'Word Worship.'" *Christianity Today* 46 (2002): 46-49.

Nichols, Anthony. "Dynamic Equivalence in Bible Translations." *Colloquium: The Australian and New Zealand Theological Review* 19 (1986): 43-53.

——. "Explicitness in Translation and the Westernization of Scripture." *Reformed Theological Review* 47, no. 3 (1988): 78-88.

——. "The Fate of 'Israel' in Recent Versions of the Bible." *In the Fullness of Time: Biblical Studies in Honour of Archbishop Donald Robinson*. Homebush West, NSW: Lancer, 1992.

Nida, Eugene A. *Toward a Science of Translating*. Leiden: Brill, 1964.

——. "Formal Correspondence in Translation." *The Bible Translator* 21, no. 3 (1970): 105-113.

——. "Translating Means Communicating: A Sociolinguistic Theory of Translation (I)." *The Bible Translator* 30, no. 1 (1979): 101-107.

——. "Translating Means Communicating: A Sociolinguistic Theory of Translation (II)." *The Bible Translator* 30, no. 3 (1979): 318-325.

Nida, Eugene A., and Charles Taber. *The Theory and Practice of Translation*. Leiden: Brill, 1982.

Omanson, Roger. "Dynamic Equivalence Translations Reconsidered." *Theological Studies* 51 (1990): 497-505.

Pascal, Blaise. *Pensées*. Translated by A. J. Krailsheimer. London: Penguin, 1995 [1670].

Plummer, Alfred. *The Epistles of St John: With Notes, Introduction and Appendices*. Cambridge Greek Testament for Schools and Colleges. Cambridge: Cambridge University Press, 1916.

Porter, Stanley E. "Some Issues in Modern Translation Theory and Study of the New Testament." *Currents in Research: Biblical Studies* 9 (2001): 350-382.

Prickett, Stephen. *Words and the Word: Language, Poetics, and Biblical Interpretation*. Cambridge: Cambridge University Press, 1986.

Publishers, Tyndale House. *Holy Bible: New Living Translation, Text and Product Preview*. Wheaton, Ill.: Tyndale House Publishers, 1996.

Punt, Jeremy. "Translating the Bible in South Africa: Challenges to Responsibility and Contextuality." Pages 94-131 in *Bible Translation on the Threshold of the Twenty-first Century*. Edited by Athalya Brenner, and Jan Willem van Henten. London: Sheffield Academic Press, 2002.

Ritchie, Daniel. "Three Recent Bible Translations: A Literary and Stylistic Perspective." *Journal of the Evangelical Theological Society* 46, no. 3 (2003): 533-545.

Roberts, J. H. "Dynamic Equivalence in Bible Translation." *Neotestamentica* 8 (1974): 7-20.

Ryken, Leland. *The Word of God in English: Criteria for Excellence in Bible Translation*. Wheaton, Ill.: Crossway, 2002.

Schmid, Hansjorg. "How to Read the First Epistle of John Non-Polemically." *Biblica* 85, no. 1 (2004): 24-41.

Schnackenburg, Rudolph. *The Johannine Epistles*. New York: Crossroad, 1992 [German 1984].

Scott, J. W. "Dynamic Equivalence and Some Theological Problems in the NIV." *Westminster Theological Journal* 48 (1986): 351-361.

Statham, Nigel. "Dynamic Equivalence and Functional Equivalence: How Do They Differ?" *The Bible Translator* 54, no. 1 (2003): 102-111.

Strauss, Mark L. "Review of Leland Ryken, *The Word of God in English*." *Journal of the Evangelical Theological Society* 46, no. 4 (2003): 738-740.

Thomson, Greg. "What Sort of Meaning Is Preserved in Translation? (I)." *Notes on Translation* 2, no. 1 (1988): 1-24.

————. "What Sort of Meaning Is Preserved in Translation? (II: Sense)." *Notes on Translation* 3, no. 1 (1989): 26-49.

————. "What Sort of Meaning Is Preserved in Translation? (III: Pragmatic meaning)." *Notes on Translation* 3, no. 4 (1989): 30-54.

————. "What Sort of Meaning Is Preserved in Translation? (IV: Presupposition)." *Notes on Translation* 4, no. 1 (1990): 21-32.

Turner, Nigel. *Style*. (Volume IV of J. H. Moulton, W. F. Howard, and N. Turner, *A Grammar of New Testament Greek*.) Edinburgh: T & T Clark, 1976.

Van Leeuwen, Raymond C. "We Really Do Need Another Bible Translation." *Christianity Today* 45, no. 13 (2001): 28-35.

————. "On Bible Translation and Hermeneutics." *After Pentecost: Language and Biblical Interpretation*. Edited by Craig Bartholomew, and Colin Greene, and Karl Moeller. Grand Rapids, Mich.: Zondervan, 2001.

Walsh, J. P. M. "Contemporary English Translations of Scripture." *Theological Studies* 50 (1989): 336-358.

————. "Dynamic or Formal Equivalence? A Response." *Theological Studies* 51 (1990): 505-508.

Wendland, Ernst. *Comparative Discourse Analysis and the Translation of Psalm 22 in Chichewa, a Bantu Language of South-Central Africa*. Lewiston: Edwin Mellen, 1993.

Westcott, Brooke Foss. *The Epistles of St John: The Greek Text with Notes and Essays*. Cambridge: Macmillan, 1892.

Wright, Benjamin G. *No Small Difference: Sirach's Relationship to Its Hebrew Parent Text*. Septuagint and Cognate Studies Series. Atlanta: Scholars, 1989.

Wright, Christopher. *God's People in God's Land*. Carlisle: Paternoster, 1997.

4

TRUTH AND FULLNESS OF MEANING:

Fullness Versus Reductionistic Semantics in Biblical Interpretation

VERN SHERIDAN POYTHRESS[1]

THE LAST THREE CENTURIES have put orthodox interpreters under pressure to show rigor and objectivity in biblical interpretation. We experience such pressure from Roman Catholic interpretation, from historical-critical interpretation, from wildly subjective and fanciful readings of the Bible, and—not least—from comparisons with the rigor, objectivity, and exactitude in modern science. But often rigor increases only by subtly ignoring or minimizing messy complexities. So let us think about complexity and richness in meaning.

Divine meaning, the meaning of God the primary author, is particularly complex,[2] but complexities abound even at the level of human authors and human readers. Theologians know that some of the main topics of Scripture display rich meaning. Think of the biblical material concerning the nature of God, the image of God, sin, Christology, and eschatology. Think also of various literary phenomena such as

---

[1] A version of this essay appeared in the *Westminster Theological Journal*. An earlier version was presented at the 56th annual meeting of the Evangelical Theological Society, San Antonio, Texas, November 18, 2004.
[2] See Vern S. Poythress, "Divine Meaning of Scripture," *Westminster Theological Journal* 48, no. 1 (1986): 241-279; Vern S. Poythress, "What Does God Say Through Human Authors?" in *Inerrancy and Hermeneutic: A Tradition, A Challenge, A Debate*, ed. Harvie M. Conn (Grand Rapids, Mich.: Baker, 1988), 81-99.

metaphor, narrative, and poetry. Think of the role of the Holy Spirit in enabling readers to appropriate the message of Scripture. All of these point to mystery, complexity, and ultimately uncontrollable richness. In contrast to this richness, exegesis in its technical forms faces some reductionistic temptations.

We may conveniently focus on the whole area of the nature of language. What view do we hold about the nature of language? What is the nature of *meaning* in language? Do we allow richness here or not? Our assumptions about language will clearly influence our approach to word meanings, sentence meanings, exegesis, and Bible translation. If we have an impoverished view of language, we are likely to have an impoverished view of the Bible as well. For example, if we think that language is designed *only* to communicate literal propositions, we will probably end up minimizing the functions of metaphor and allusions. If we think that language is designed *only* to talk about *this* world, we will be suspicious of God-talk as an allegedly improper use.

ORIGINS OF LANGUAGE

Our challenges increase because of some unhealthy pressures deriving from the surrounding culture. To begin with, evolutionary modes of thinking would like to trace language back to animal cries and calls. According to this kind of thinking, just as man has gradually ascended from the slime, human language has gradually ascended from grunts. Modern language, like modern human anatomy, finds its original essence in providing for survival. This mode of thinking naturally throws suspicion on all use of human language for nonmaterial goals. The most material and simplest meaning is the most basic. Talk about God obviously stretches, perhaps to the breaking point, the original functions of language.

By contrast, the Bible shows that human language from the beginning included the function of serving for communication between God and man (Gen. 1:28-30; 2:16-18). Speech about God and speech from God does not represent a stretch, but a normal function of human language.

For example, God is the first and principal ruler over the world. Human beings created in the image of God become subordinate rulers.

The creation of human beings according to the plan of God produces an analogical relation between God's rulership and human rule. God is king in the supreme sense, while human kings mirror his rule on a subordinate level. To call God *king* is not "mere" metaphor, in the sense of being unreal. It affirms a real analogy between God and man. It involves a normal function for human language.

Moreover, it is plain from Scripture that God designed language in such a way that there can be multi-dimensional, complex, nuanced communication between God and man. God can tell stories, both fictional (parables) and nonfictional. He can expound and reason theologically, as in Romans, and he can express the full range of human emotions, as in the Psalms. The Bible contains propositional truth, but can express it either in prose or in poetry. It contains both short sayings, as in Proverbs, and multi-generational histories, as in Genesis. The meaning of one sentence in Genesis coheres with the meanings in the whole narrative. Meaning is not reducible to pellet-sized isolated sentences that are thrown together at random.

For example, Genesis 12:2 says, "I will make of you a great nation." The meaning of that sentence can be determined only if we know who "I" and "you" are, which depends on the immediate context. And the full meaning of "great nation" can be seen only as the promise begins to find fulfillment near the end of Genesis and into Exodus. And what do we do with a more loaded term like "blessing"? "I will bless you and make your name great, so that you will be a blessing," Genesis says (Gen. 12:2). This promise contrasts subtly with the earlier arrogant attempt at Babel where people desired to "make a name for ourselves" (Gen. 11:4). And it resonates with the later instances of blessing that run all the way through the Old Testament and into the New. All this is fairly obvious to a reasonably skilled reader. But we must now ask whether modern theories of meaning are adequate to capture this richness.

So let us look at three technical tools that have blossomed in the twentieth century: symbolic logic, structural linguistics, and translation theory. All three contribute to understanding language, but at the same time, when clumsily used, threaten to reduce meaning to one dimension.

SYMBOLIC LOGIC

Reflection about logic goes all the way back to Aristotle. But formal symbolic logic blossomed in the late nineteenth and early twentieth century with the work of Gottlob Frege, Bertrand Russell, and others.[3] Symbolic logic made more rigorous the idea of a valid proof. And it proves useful in uncovering logical fallacies in informal reasoning. But what of its limitations? For the most part, the use of mathematical logic requires that we begin with isolated sentences. This step already involves a reduction of the full richness of human communication as it occurs in long discourses and social interaction. It also requires that a sentence be isolated from its situational context. It then treats the sentence almost wholly in terms of its truth value.

Modern evangelicalism has rightly insisted on propositional revelation in Scripture in response to liberal and neo-orthodox reductions of revelation to religious feeling and personal encounter. But in the process, we must beware of the reverse problem of reducing the discourse of Scripture merely to its truth value. It does have truth value. But the meaning of a whole discourse or of one sentence within it includes *more* than the fact that it is either true or false. It is related in meaning to many other parts of Scripture; it asks for application in our lives; it has the power to transform our hearts; and so on.

Symbolic logic is so obviously reductive in its approach to meaning that perhaps we do not need so much to remind ourselves of its reductive character. So let us pass on to the second great area of advance, structural linguistics.[4]

SIMPLIFICATIONS IN STRUCTURAL LINGUISTICS

As with symbolic logic, so with linguistics: we need to appreciate the value of linguistics, but also become aware of built-in limitations. Human language is so complicated and multi-dimensional that simplifications had to be made in order to get structural linguistics started. But it is easy along the way, in the excitement of discovery, to forget those

[3] For an introduction, see Susanne K. K. Langer, *An Introduction to Symbolic Logic* (New York: Dover, 1953); Irving M. Copi, *Introduction to Logic*, 4th ed. (New York: Macmillan, 1972).

[4] Structural linguistics, as a twentieth-century discipline, is here distinguished from historical linguistics (diachronic linguistics), which has a much longer history, and from earlier attempts at grammatical and phonetic analysis of a single language.

simplifications and to make exaggerated or one-sided claims about the implications.

In considering the development of structural linguistics, I will have to make some simplifications myself and confine myself to some high points illustrating the trends.[5] I focus particularly on the issue of how linguistics treats *meaning.*

Ferdinand de Saussure, 1906–1911

Many consider that structural linguistics had its origin in the lectures of Ferdinand de Saussure in 1906–1907, 1908–1909, and 1910–1911, which were later compiled into the book *Course in General Linguistics.*[6] After some historical observations, Saussure introduced the main body of discussion by delineating the object of linguistics. Linguistics will study language (*langue*) as a system, instead of studying speech (*parole*). That is, it will study the systematic regularities common to all native speakers, rather than the particularities of every individual speech by every individual speaker. For example, the verb tenses in English, the present tense ("I go"), the past tense ("I went"), the future tense ("I will go"), and so on, are one of the systematic regularities. An utterance using the past tense of the verb "to go" ("He *went* to town yesterday.") is a particularity, an instance of *parole.*

In the light of hindsight this famous move toward focusing on the system of language decisively contributed to the delineation of linguistics as a subject distinct from textual analysis and exegesis. But the advance came with a cost. Any reasonable approach to the meaning of a specific communication (*parole*) must take into account the speaker, the audience, and the circumstances, since all three affect the nuances of a particular speech or text. The meaning of a particular utterance naturally depends on the particular words and their meanings. But it is not simply a mechanical product of word meanings, but includes a complex particular texture that varies with circumstance. The expression, "The door is open," could be a simple assertion of fact. But a detective could

---

[5] See the historical accounts in Leonard Bloomfield, *Language* (London: George Allen & Unwin, 1933), 4-19; Peter Matthews, *A Short History of Structural Linguistics* (Cambridge: Cambridge University Press, 2001).

[6] Ferdinand de Saussure, *Course in General Linguistics* (New York/Toronto/London: McGraw-Hill, 1959).

be implying that it is a significant clue to solving a mystery. An angry person could use the expression to indicate indirectly that the person he addresses should get out. Saussure deliberately cut off the variations in order to study "the system."

Second, Saussure largely cut off the influence of syntagmatic context (that is, textual context) by focusing on word-meanings.[7] Like the earlier moves, this one flattens out the complexity of meaning. In later discussion he added context back in with the distinction between syntagmatic and associative (or paradigmatic) relations.[8] But the damage has been done, since the consideration of syntagms still relies on words as its starting point. In many ways this reduction is quite understandable, perhaps in some sense necessary, because words are stable in relation to the surrounding speech (*parole*), and one must start with some simplifications if one is to get linguistics off the ground.

Third, Saussure introduced a model for linguistic signs with three parts: the "sound-image" or signifier, the "concept" or signified, and the "sign" that consists of both parts together. For example, the word *arbor* in Latin associates the concept of tree with the sound-image of a sequence a+r+b+o+r.[9] The meaning we may associate with the concept, while the form consists in the sound-image. This move makes sense as a way of defining more rigorously the distinction between form and meaning. But it introduces a subtle reductionism in the thinking about meaning. Children learning a language often learn the meanings of words through their occurrences in social situations where there is reference to a real-world object. Words for milk and soup, cat and dog come to have meaning through the help of occurrences of milk and soup and cats and dogs in the environment. In the long run, referential functions have an indispensable role in meaning. Saussure has left out reference, and settled on "concept," which suggest a purely mental phenomenon. This restriction is once again understandable, given his earlier decision to focus on the language system. The language system does not directly refer to objects in the world in the same way that spe-

---

[7] Ibid., 65, "The Nature of the Linguistic Sign."
[8] Ibid., 124-127.
[9] Ibid., 65.

cific speakers refer to such objects in specific speeches (*parole*). But one can never understand meaning in its fullness if one leaves out reference.

The omission of reference offers an open door for later reductionisms, as one can see with the case of certain forms of structuralism in which language is treated as a closed system of signs that refer only to other signs. In the hands of certain practitioners, the "meaning" of any one particular text got reduced to the central truth that meaning is a function of system.

Saussure proposed still another reduction when he shifted from "meaning" to "value." By "value" he means the significance that a particular unit has by virtue of its oppositions or contrasts to neighboring units. He says, "Language is a system of interdependent terms in which the value of each term results solely from the simultaneous presence of the others."[10] The word "solely" signals the reduction. One will thereby ignore both reference and the historical accumulation of potential for literary allusion to earlier occurrences of the same expression. The benefits of focusing on the system of oppositions are now well known and undeniable. But we should not conceal from ourselves that these benefits derive partly from ignoring intractable complexities in what is left out.

Leonard Bloomfield, 1933

A second milestone in the development of structural linguistics occurred with Leonard Bloomfield's publication of *Language* in 1933.[11] Like Saussure, Bloomfield considered the correlation between sound and meaning to be fundamental.[12] And initially he introduced meaning in connection with life situations in which language is used to accomplish practical tasks. But simplifications entered in as he focused on the concerns of linguistics. For one thing, Bloomfield used a simple stimulus-response model for understanding human behavior.[13] He states bluntly, ". . . in all sciences like linguistics, which observe some specific type of human activity, the worker must proceed exactly as if he held the materialistic view."[14]

---

[10] Ibid., 114. On the same page Saussure explicitly distinguishes "value" from "signification." Likewise he says, "In a language-state everything is based on relations" (122).

[11] Bloomfield, *Language* (see note 5, above).

[12] Ibid., 27.

[13] Ibid., 23-31, 33-34.

[14] Ibid., 38.

Though Bloomfield in his early discussion equated meaning with the entire situation in which an utterance occurs, he soon reduced the task to "constant and definite meaning" for any one form.[15] This move—again an understandable and convenient simplification to facilitate early progress in linguistics—ignores the influence of context. Meaning is effectively reduced to the meaning of an expression that is independent of the larger context.

Noam Chomsky, 1957

As our next milestone we may conveniently take Noam Chomsky's *Syntactic Structures* in 1957.[16] Chomsky's book laid the foundation for what came to be known as *generative grammar*. Together with the later work *Aspects of the Theory of Syntax*,[17] this book had enormous influence on the direction of linguistic research, because of its appeal to rigor and formalization, and because of the impressive conclusion that certain simple types of formal grammar were provably inadequate for the complexities of natural language.

But rigor and formalization came, as usual, with a price. Chomsky stipulated that a *language* was "a set (finite or infinite) of sentences, each finite in length and constructed out of a finite set of elements."[18] This definition, which allows for a language to be subjected to a rigorous mathematically based analysis of syntax, ignores the role of context, both the context of a situation and the context of a discourse in paragraphs and larger sections. It is a vast simplification, but unfortunately Chomsky did not overtly acknowledge how much it simplifies. In the next sentence after this definition, he simply declared that, "All natural languages in their spoken or written form are languages in this sense, . . ." We also hear hints that grammaticality is independent of meaning, which is true only as a first approximation.[19] In the long run, grammatical categories make sense only in the service of meaningful communication.

---

[15] Ibid., 158.

[16] Noam Chomsky, *Syntactic Structures* (The Hague: Mouton, 1957). The copy to which I have access is the second printing in 1962.

[17] Noam Chomsky, *Aspects of the Theory of Syntax* (Cambridge, Mass.: MIT Press, 1965).

[18] Chomsky, *Syntactic Structures,* 13. Chomsky also assumed that the sequences fall neatly into *grammatical* and *ungrammatical* types, which he acknowledged is an idealization (14). To achieve the impressive formal result of showing that finite state grammars are inadequate for natural language, he also had to introduce the idealization that says that sentences may be indefinitely complex—though in fact the limitations of human memory disallow in practice sentences of a million words (23).

[19] Ibid., 15; see also the more extended discussion on pages 92-105.

Chomsky also introduced the significant distinction between *kernel* sentences and nonkernel sentences.[20] Kernel sentences are simple, active-voice sentences like *The boy fed the dog*. These sentences arise within Chomsky's formalism by the application of phrase structure rules and obligatory transformations. Nonkernel sentences include passive sentences, such as "The dog was fed by the boy," and derived expressions like "It was the boy who fed the dog." One must also consider expressions like "The boy's feeding the dog." The sentence "I was reassured by the boy's feeding the dog" derives from two distinct kernel sentences, namely "The boy fed the dog" and "It reassured me." All complex sentences, as well as other sentence types that derive from two or more kernel sentences, arise from applying optional transformational rules to the original set of kernel sentences.[21]

This schema opens the door to the possibility of a semantic analysis in which the meaning of a sentence is the sum of the meanings of the kernel sentences from which it is derived, plus the semantic relations between kernels that are specified by the grammatical links between them. Such an analysis is tempting precisely because in many cases it approximates the truth, and captures some of the core meaning or basic meaning that we associate with a sentence. But as a total account of meaning it is obviously reductionistic.

Linguistics has continued to develop since the Chomskyan revolution in 1957 and 1965. Chomsky's generative grammar eventually mutated into the theory of government and binding, and then into the minimalist program.[22] Though the detailed structure of the theories has changed markedly, the spirit of formalization and reductionism remains in place. But we also see challenges from competing theories. Cognitive linguistics with its meaning-centered approach challenges the grammar-centered approach of generative grammar and its successors.[23] Other

---

[20] Ibid., 45.

[21] Technically, the optional transformations are applied to "forms that underlie kernel sentences . . . or prior transforms" (ibid.).

[22] See, for example, Noam Chomsky, *Lectures on Government and Binding* (Dordrecht/Cinnaminson, N.J.: Foris, 1981); Noam Chomsky, *Some Concepts and Consequences of the Theory of Government and Binding* (Cambridge, Mass.: MIT Press, 1982); Liliane Haegeman, *Introduction to Government and Binding Theory* (Oxford: Blackwell, 1991); Andrew Radford, *Syntax: A Minimalist Introduction* (Cambridge: Cambridge University Press, 1997); David Adger, *Core Syntax: A Minimalist Approach* (Oxford: Oxford University Press, 2003).

[23] See, for example, David Lee, *Cognitive Linguistics: An Introduction* (Oxford: Oxford University Press, 2002).

alternative linguistic theories continue to attract followers.[24] Semantic theory has attracted continuing interest, sometimes without any strong dependence on a particular theory of grammar or phonology.[25] The possibility of coherent alternative theoretical approaches suggests that any one approach is selective (and therefore potentially reductionistic) in its understanding.[26]

TRANSLATION THEORY: EUGENE NIDA

In the twentieth century a theory of Bible translation developed in tandem with linguistics and tried to profit in a multitude of ways from the developments in structural linguistics.[27] But while linguistics initially focused largely on issues of phonology and grammar, translation had to deal directly with meaning and all its complexities. Bible translators confronted the task of translating into thousands of third-world tribal languages. Eugene Nida, in consultation with other pioneers in the field, developed the theory of "dynamic equivalence" or "functional equivalence," which stressed the importance of transferring meaning, not grammatical form.[28] Nida discussed various kinds of complexity in meaning even at a comparatively early date, beginning with his 1947 publication of *Bible Translating*.[29] He explicitly spoke about translating "fullest meaning" instead of a bare minimum.[30]

In 1964, Nida published the fuller and more theoretically advanced work *Toward a Science of Translating*.[31] By this time, he was aware of the formalistic approach in generative grammar, not only Chomsky's

---

[24] See, for example, Mary Dalrymple, *Lexical-Functional Grammar* (San Diego: Academic Press, 2001); René Kager, *Optimality Theory* (Cambridge: Cambridge University Press, 1999). And I believe there is still value in the more nonformalized, discovery-oriented, antireductive approach of tagmemic theory (Kenneth L. Pike, *Linguistic Concepts: An Introduction to Tagmemics* [Lincoln: University of Nebraska Press, 1982]).

[25] See John Lyons, *Semantics,* 2 vols. (Cambridge: Cambridge University Press, 1977); D. Alan Cruse, *Meaning in Language: An Introduction to Semantics and Pragmatics* (Oxford: Oxford University Press, 2000).

[26] See Pike, *Linguistic Concepts,* 5-9, on the role of theory in language analysis.

[27] For a broader context, see L. G. Kelly, *The True Interpreter: A History of Translation Theory and Practice in the West* (New York: St. Martin's, 1979).

[28] See the discussion in Vern S. Poythress and Wayne A. Grudem, *The Gender-Neutral Bible Controversy: Muting the Masculinity of God's Words* (Nashville: Broadman & Holman, 2000), 57-90.

[29] Eugene Nida, *Bible Translating* (New York: American Bible Society, 1947).

[30] Ibid., 23.

[31] Eugene A. Nida, *Toward a Science of Translating: With Special Reference to Principles Involved in Bible Translating* (Leiden: Brill, 1964).

Syntactic Structures, but also Katz and Fodor's ground-breaking article, "The Structure of a Semantic Theory."[32] Nevertheless, in the first three chapters of his book he refused to be reductionistic. He spoke explicitly about many dimensions of meaning, and referred favorably to Roman Jakobson's classification of meaning into emotive, conative, referential, poetic, phatic, and metalingual dimensions.[33] He was so bold as to say:

> . . . no word ever has precisely the same meaning twice, for each speech event is in a sense unique, involving participants who are constantly changing and referents which are never fixed. Bloomfield (1933, 407) describes this problem by saying that "every utterance of a speech form involves a minute semantic innovation."[34]

And again:

> In any discussion of communication and meaning, one must recognize at the start, each source and each receptor differs from all others, not only in the way the formal aspects of the language are handled, but also in the manner in which symbols are used to designate certain referents. If, as is obviously true, each person employs language on the basis of his background and no two individuals ever have precisely the same background, then it is also obvious that no two persons ever mean exactly the same thing by the use of the same language symbols. At the same time, however, there is an amazing degree of similarity in the use of language. . . .[35]

But Nida was also determined to use whatever insights he could obtain from Chomsky's generative grammar. So in chapter 4 he focused on what he called "linguistic meaning." Here he looked at the meanings associated with distribution of a word within larger contexts and within grammatical structures.[36] According to Nida, linguistic meaning often appears on "two levels":

---

[32] Jerrold J. Katz and Jerry Fodor, "The Structure of a Semantic Theory," *Language* 39 (1963): 170-210.
[33] Nida, *Toward a Science of Translating,* 40-46. Page 45n.3 refers to Roman Jakobson, "Linguistics and Poetics," in *Style in Language,* ed. Thomas A. Sebeok (Cambridge, Mass.: Technology Press, MIT, 1960), 350-377.
[34] Nida, *Toward a Science of Translating,* 48.
[35] Ibid., 51.
[36] The initial discussion of "linguistic meaning" occurs in ibid., 41-42.

First, that meaning which is derived from the kernel construction by way of the transformations, and secondly that meaning which is supplied by the particular terminal construction (the end result in the process of transformation from the kernel to the resulting expression).[37]

In using the key terms *kernel* and *transformations,* Nida was clearly adopting the framework of Chomsky's generative grammar. Meaning was now to be seen within this framework.[38]

The concentration on "linguistic meaning" involves a reduction. Nida was aware of this, and so in the following chapter he supplemented this account with a discussion of "referential and emotive meanings."[39] But someone less aware than Nida can easily use the schema reductionistically to think that all or almost all of the really significant meaning is linguistic meaning, and that this meaning comes to light exclusively through the Chomskyan framework. The temptation is all the stronger because Nida himself suggested that his scheme could serve as the basis for a translation procedure:

> . . . it is most efficient for us to develop an approach to translation which takes these facts fully into consideration. Instead of attempting to set up transfers from one language to another by working out long series of equivalent formal structures which are presumably adequate to "translate" from one language into another, it is both scientifically and practically more efficient (1) to reduce the source text to its structurally simplest and most semantically evident kernels, (2) to transfer the meaning from source language to receptor language on a structurally simple level, and (3) to generate the stylistically and semantically equivalent expression in the receptor language.[40]

As Nida indicates in the surrounding discussion, an approach of this type looks promising particularly for languages whose formal (grammatical) structures do not match well with those of Indo-European lan-

---

[37] Ibid., 65.

[38] The terminology occurs also in Eugene A. Nida and Charles R. Taber, *The Theory and Practice of Translation* (Leiden: Brill, 1969), 39.

[39] Nida, *Toward a Science of Translating,* 70-119; note the earlier delineation of kinds of meaning on pages 41-43; see also Nida and Taber, *Theory and Practice of Translation,* 56-98.

[40] Nida, *Toward a Science of Translating,* 68. One can see the three-stage process worked out more explicitly and practically in Nida and Taber, *Theory and Practice of Translation,* 104.

guages such as English, German, Greek, and Latin. All languages show "remarkably similar kernel structures."[41] So if we can decompose meaning into these kernels, we can transfer it more easily from one language to another. In addition, the nonkernel structures do not necessarily reveal directly the underlying semantic relations. For example, the sentence "he hit the man with a stick"[42] may mean either that he used the stick as an instrument, or that the man who received the blow had a stick in hand. Such ambiguous constructions often have to be translated differently depending on the underlying meaning. Nida therefore proposed a three-stage process, in which the first stage involves decomposition into underlying kernel meanings.

The three-stage process promises benefits. But it comes at the cost of leaving out much of the richness of meaning that Nida expounded in the immediately preceding chapter. We have a breathtaking reduction here. Let us list some of its features.

First, we engage in reduction by ignoring all the idiosyncrasies of an individual speaker.

Second, we reduce meaning to the meaning of sentences, and no longer consider the interaction with situational context or the larger textual context of discourse. It should be noted in Nida's favor that elsewhere he explicitly called for attention to the larger contexts of paragraphs and discourse.[43] But this sound advice of his is at odds with the transformational generative model of his day, which confined its analysis to the sentence and its constituents. The reduction to considering only sentence meaning, and to considering sentences one by one, leads to ignoring discourse cohesion, including cohesion achieved through the repetition of key words. This reduction then inhibits the reader from seeing meaning relations not only within individual books of the Bible, but in later allusions to earlier passages. The important theme of promise and fulfillment is damaged.

Third, we reduce all figurative expressions to a literal level, since the

---

[41] Nida, *Toward a Science of Translating*, 68.

[42] An example used in ibid., 61.

[43] . . . expert translators and linguists have been able to demonstrate that the individual sentence in turn is not enough. The focus should be on the paragraph, and to some extent on the total discourse" (Nida and Taber, *Theory and Practice of Translation*, 102).

core formal structures in transformational generative grammar deal only with literal meanings.

Fourth, we reduce meaning from a richness including referential, emotive, expressive, and other dimensions to the single plane of "linguistic meaning."

Fifth, we assume that meanings in the original are all clear and transparent. This assumption may be approximately true with some types of source texts on technical subjects or on mundane affairs; but it is far from being true with the Bible, which contains both obscurities and depths.[44]

Sixth, we reduce the meaning of a complex nonkernel sentence to its constituent kernels.[45] This move is a genuine reduction, since meanings in fact do not reduce in a simple way to the meanings of kernel structures. Consider the expression, "God's love." Can we reduce this expression to the kernel structure "God loves you"? In many contexts, this involves a decided change of meaning, since the expression "God's love" does not indicate the object of his love. Supplying an object such as "you" or "people," as we must do in a kernel sentence, forces upon us greater definiteness than the original expression.[46]

A similar problem often occurs with passives. "Bill was overwhelmed" is less definite than "Something overwhelmed Bill." For one thing, the passive expression does not indicate whether or not some one particular thing did the overwhelming. Maybe Bill felt overwhelmed, but there was no easily identifiable source for the feeling. Or maybe some other person, rather than some circumstance, overwhelmed Bill. The running back charged into him and overwhelmed him on the football field.

Similar problems occur when the back-transformation into a kernel requires us to supply an object. For example, the expression "Charlotte's kiss" gets transformed into the kernel sentence "Charlotte kissed someone." But did she kiss her dog? The "someone" in question may be an animal rather than a human being. The word *someone* does

---

[44] The point about depth versus transparency is made eloquently by Stephen Prickett, *Words and the Word* (Cambridge: Cambridge University Press, 1986), 4-36.

[45] Compare Chomsky, *Aspects of the Theory of Syntax*, 132.

[46] Still another problem exists with an expression like "the love of God." This expression may indicate either the love that God has toward someone, or the love that someone has toward God, depending on the context. And some contexts may deliberately play on the potential ambiguity.

not then represent the possibilities quite adequately. Or did she throw a kiss to a large audience? Or did she just make a kissing sound, without directing her lips toward any particular someone? If we produce a kernel sentence to represent meaning, we expect it to have an object. But with any object we supply, such as "someone," we change the meaning by introducing assumptions that are not contained in the vaguer expression, "Charlotte's kiss." (Generative grammar in 1965 could potentially handle some of this kind of complexity using so-called "subcategorization rules." But such rules are still an abstraction that exists several steps away from the particular changes in meaning-nuances that one may observe in actual sentences in natural languages.)

The reduction arises partly from reductive moves that have already taken place within the theory of transformational generative grammar, which Nida was using as a model. But they also occur because somewhere along the line people may begin to assume that the transformations in question are meaning-preserving. They actually change meaning, as Nida admitted when he talked about "two levels of linguistic meaning," the second of which is "supplied by the particular terminal construction."[47] Moreover, from a semantic point of view, the speaker does not necessarily start psychologically with a kernel sentence.[48] The speaker may not know or may not be concerned to supply semantically absent information that would have to be supplied in order to construct a kernel structure.

In fact, generative grammar originated as an attempt to describe grammar, not meaning. It so happened that generative transformations connected sentences with analogous meanings. But no one could guarantee that the meanings would be identical. Sometimes differences in meaning are obvious. Compare the question, "Did you feed the dog?" with the analogous statement, "You fed the dog." These two are transformationally related. But they differ in meaning because one is a question. By that very fact it has a different function in communication than the corresponding statement.

To insist that the meanings must be identical constitutes a reduc-

---

[47] Nida, *Toward a Science of Translating*, 65.
[48] In fact, Chomsky warned against understanding generative grammar as a psychological theory (Chomsky, *Aspects of the Theory of Syntax*, 9).

tion.[49] It may still be a useful reduction. The linguist who uses the reductive process achieves rigor and insight of various kinds. But he also puts himself and his disciples in a position where they may forget the reduction, or refuse to acknowledge it. They then force meaning in human discourse to match their "scientific" results, rather than forcing their science to acknowledge the full reality of human communication.

Scientific Rigor

The occurrence of the words "science" and "scientific" in the discussions can also signal a problem. Many have observed that in the twentieth century social scientists have often envied the rigor and prestige of natural sciences, and have struggled to achieve the same level of rigor within their own fields. But a field dealing with human beings contains innate complexities and multi-dimensional relationalities. In such a situation, rigor and fullness of meaning will often be like two ends of a seesaw. If one goes up, the other must go down.[50]

Nida's 1964 book shows some telltale symptoms of this problem. He entitles the book *Toward a Science of Translating*. Its title already introduces a tension: will we have "science," so-called, with its ever-increasing rigor? If so, will we put ourselves at odds with the centuries-

---

[49] There are complexities about how we might treat transformations. In *Syntactic Structures* (1957) Chomsky postulated a simple system of phrase structure rules leading to a relatively simple set of kernel sentences. Under this schema, questions were to be derived from statements by applying the optional transformation "T_q" (63). But by 1965 Chomsky had incorporated the question marker into the base structure, and the question transformation became obligatory, so that a transformation analogous to T_q could preserve the additional meaning involved in asking a question (see Chomsky, *Aspects of the Theory of Syntax*, 132).

Obviously over a period of time one can incorporate more and more previously neglected meaning aspects into the base grammar, in hopes of achieving a more adequate account of meaning. But the cost is increasing complexity in the base. In the limit, one might imagine a situation where all the lost meaning has been reintegrated; but the cost would likely be a horrendous complexity. In fact, for the sake of rigorous testability, generative grammar chooses in spirit to seek reduction rather than fullness of meaning.

In 1964 Nida did not fully endorse Chomsky's later (1965) view that transformations must be meaning-preserving. Whether because he was working with Chomsky's 1957 view in *Syntactic Structures* or because he saw the reductionism inherent in generative grammar, he affirmed that some extra meaning is contributed by the "particular terminal construction" (*Toward a Science of Translating*, 65). But if so, it vitiates the attempt to translate by reducing meaning to the underlying kernel structures (as Nida proposed in *Toward a Science of Translating*, 68).

[50] Kelly delineates the problem: "Linguists' models assume that translation is essentially transmission of data, while hermeneutic theorists take it to be an interpretative re-creation of text. It is hardly surprising then, that each group, sure that it has the whole truth, lives in isolation from the other" (Kelly, *True Interpreter*, 34).

old philological and hermeneutical instinct that interpretation and translation alike are arts, not sciences?

Yes, we may have maxims for interpretation or translation. At points, we may have highly technical procedures for checking out our instincts, and for searching ever more minutely the meaning of particular words in particular contexts, and the meanings of various grammatical constructions. But in the end the process of translation is so complex and multi-dimensional that it must remain an art; it involves technique to be sure, as all good art does, but it is never reducible to a merely mechanical or formal process.[51]

Now Nida's title does not say, "The Science of Translating," but "*Toward* a Science of Translating." The word "toward" signals that we are still feeling our way. We have not yet arrived at a full-fledged science. But the title nevertheless holds out as a goal the reduction of translation to science. And this, I would allege, contains a built-in bias in favor of formalism, and with it an invitation to move toward a reductionist approach toward meaning. It suggests in particular that all figurative, allusive, and metaphorical language must be reduced to the level of the literal, in order to be fit for processing by the scientific machinery.

Am I merely imagining sinister connotations that Nida did not intend? I do not propose to speculate about his inner intentions. Moreover, I have already indicated that Nida displays in his chapter 3 a great deal of sensitivity and understanding concerning the multi-dimensional character of the meaning of texts. The problem, if you will, is not with Nida's own personal awareness of meaning, but with the program he proposes to others—others who may be less aware of the complexities.

One can see the problem coming to life as one contemplates Nida's description of translation after his discussion of generative grammar and kernel sentences:

> Instead of attempting to set up transfers from one language to another by working out long series of equivalent formal structures which are presumably adequate to "translate" from one language

---

[51] Note the duality that Kelly sees in theories of translation: "For the majority, translation is a literary craft. . . . In contrast, linguists and grammarians have identified theory with analysis of semantic and grammatical operations" (Kelly, *True Interpreter*, 2).

into another, it is both scientifically and practically more efficient (1) to reduce the source text to its structurally simplest and most semantically evident kernels, (2) to transfer the meaning from source language to receptor language on a structurally simple level, and (3) to generate the stylistically and semantically equivalent expression in the receptor language.[52]

This key sentence contrasts two kinds of approach, both of which are utterly *formalistic* and mechanical about the translation process. The first approach would match surface grammatical structures between two languages, using an interminably long list. The second approach matches underlying kernels instead of surface structures.

But Nida has here presupposed that the only alternative to one formalistic approach is another formalistic one. He has not even mentioned the possibility of an *art*—the art of translation.[53] What if we have someone translate who has a high level of comprehension of complex meanings in both languages? He does not translate merely by mechanical application of formal rules. Rather, using solid knowledge, artistry, and intuition together, he comes up with a translation that captures more fully the total meaning of the original. Is not this nonformal, nonmechanistic approach superior to both of Nida's alternatives? Nida in his excitement over the potential of linguistics has lost sight of the complementary perspectives offered in the centuries-long traditions of hermeneutical theorists and literary theorists.[54]

The inclusion of the word "scientifically" in the middle of Nida's sentence increases the problem. It biases readers to understand translation as a formal, mechanical process. It suggests that once the appropriate transformational rules are known for the two languages in

---

[52] Nida, *Toward a Science of Translating*, 68.
[53] Further down on the same page (ibid.) Nida mentions "the really competent translator," by which he presumably means someone who knows both languages intimately. But Nida uses this temporary tip of the hat toward competence only as evidence that restructuring is sometimes legitimate; he does not consider whether the existence of this competent translator also shows the limitations in the reductionism and formalism that Nida proposes everywhere else on the page.
[54] See Kelly, *True Interpreter*, 2-4, 36. "In the polemic between these three groups of theorists, only a few individuals have perceived that their approaches are complementary" (3-4). "Where linguistics concentrates on the means of expression, the complementary hermeneutic approach analyses the goal of linguistic interactions. The focus here is anti-empiricist: the central reality is not the observable expression, but the understanding of the cognitive and affective levels of language through which communication takes place" (7).

question, one simply applies the mechanical process in order to produce the appropriate result.

I do not want to be too hard on Nida. Nida is partly thinking of the practical constraints on Bible translations into exotic languages. The professionally trained missionary Bible translator cannot hope to have the native speaker's competence in Mazotec or Quechua. Given the translator's limitations, thinking in terms of kernel sentences and transformations can provide genuine insights into differences between languages, and suggest ways in which the verses of Scripture may have to be re-expressed in a particular language.

But, as Nida stresses elsewhere, there is no good substitute for testing a proposed translation with native speakers.[55] One must take into account the full effects of connotative and affective meanings, of context, of previous enculturation, and so on. There can be no *science* of translation in the strict sense, and Nida's own practical discussions are proof of it. The formalization of meaning constitutes a danger, because it can lead to a reductionistic approach to translation by those who do not see the partial and one-sided character of Nida's proposed procedure. A wide human sensitivity and comprehension is needed, and this larger human involvement complements technical study of language and linguistics.[56] And I should underline the complementarity here. The technical study of language and linguistics does have much to contribute. I am not advocating an ignorance of linguistics, or a minimization of its value, but an awareness of the specialized character of its foci, and the consequent limitations in the vision of any one linguistic approach.

In considering Nida's approach and its subsequent development, one must also bear in mind the practical limitations that arise in many situations where the target for Bible translation is a tribal culture. Cultures with no previous knowledge of the Bible or Christianity, and sometimes with little or no previous knowledge of worldwide cultures, create special difficulties for communicating religious truths. The extra barriers put a heavy premium on making everything simple and clear. Without this simplicity—which itself constitutes a kind of reduction— the target readers, with minimal skills in literacy, may give up altogether

---

[55] Nida and Taber, *Theory and Practice of Translation*, 163-182.
[56] Kelly notes the complementarity in *True Interpreter*, 3-4.

and not read the Bible at all. One can sympathize with the goals of utmost simplicity and clarity in such cases without converting these goals into general standards for Bible translation or for discourse meaning and semantics.

Componential Analysis of Meaning

One can see a similar encroachment of reductionism in the componential analysis of meaning. In the approach called componential analysis, the meaning of a word gets reduced to a series of binary components. A "bachelor" is (1) human, (2) male, and (3) unmarried. We may express this result by providing a list of three binary components: [+ human], [+ male], and [- married]. Componential analysis has a considerable history in the area of phonology. Here it works reasonably and insightfully, because phonology deals with a small, limited system of sounds whose significance depends largely on contrasts with other elements in the system. Thus in English the phoneme /p/ is distinguished from /b/ by the role of the vocal chords, and from /f/ and /v/ by the fact that the air stream is at one point completely stopped. We say that /p/ is [- voiced] (unvoiced) and [+ stop]. In keeping with its formalistic and reductionistic program, generative grammar soon adopted the use of componential analysis in its study of meaning. By analogy with the procedure of decomposing phonemes into distinctive binary phonological features, we now decompose meanings into distinctive binary meaning components such as [+ male] or [- married].

When we deal with kinship terms and certain other well-defined, limited areas of meanings,[57] an analysis into meaning components may yield significant insight. And it may be of value more broadly for the language learner who is trying to appreciate key meaning contrasts in a new language. Nida rightly saw the value and introduced "componential analysis" of meaning in connection with his instruction about translation.[58] But Nida also indicated some limitations:

---

[57] Modern linguistic theory speaks of "semantic domains" or "semantic fields." See, for example, John Lyons, *Semantics* (Cambridge: Cambridge University Press, 1977), 1:250-269. For an application to Greek lexicography, see Johannes P. Louw and Eugene A. Nida, *Greek-English Lexicon of the New Testament Based on Semantic Domains*, 2 vols. (New York: United Bible Societies, 1988). For an example with kinship terms, see Nida, *Toward a Science of Translating*, 90-93.

[58] Ibid., 82-87.

By analyzing only the minimal features of distinctiveness, many supplementary and connotative elements of meaning are disregarded, . . . [59]

The danger here is that careless practitioners may later overlook the reductionistic character of componential analysis, and consider it to be *the definitive* statement about meaning.

The reductionism in componential analysis can get added to other reductionisms that we have observed in Nida's use of kernel sentences. As a result, reductionistic approaches to meaning may enter the process of Bible translation. Anthony H. Nichols, in his extended analysis of dynamic equivalence translation, has shown that dangers of this kind are not merely hypothetical, but have had a baleful effect on some translations.[60]

Unfortunately, the formalistic, "scientific" cast of the theory may make it difficult to take criticism. We know, do we not, that science is superior to the rabble's naivete? Once we have a scientific theory, criticism from outside can easily be dismissed as uninformed, because it does not bow before the power and insight of the theory. Theorists have then discovered a means for self-protection. When an outside observer complains about losses of meaning in a sample translation,[61] he may be told that he is not competent to judge, because he is not initiated into the mysteries of componential analysis and translation theory. What the translation theorist's net does not catch is summarily judged not to be fish!

Decades ago, Bible translators learned the maxim that one must listen carefully to the judgments of native speakers about meaning. It would be ironic if now, as translation theory grows more mature, it were used in reverse to pronounce "expert" judgments about which kinds of meaning native speakers may be allowed to worry about.

---

[59] Ibid., 87; other limitations are listed on the same page.

[60] Anthony Howard Nichols, "Translating the Bible: A Critical Analysis of E. A. Nida's Theory of Dynamic Equivalence and Its Impact upon Recent Bible Translations," Ph.D. dissertation, University of Sheffield, 1996. As one might have guessed from the nature of Nida's dynamic equivalence model, one of the effects is a flattening or elimination of figurative speech. Figurative speech poses a genuine challenge for translation, because a word-for-word rendering of a figure into another language may be difficult to understand or may invite misunderstanding. But this is not to say that we must go to the opposite extreme and systematically eliminate figurative expressions because of an aversion to anything that is not transparently clear.

[61] For an eloquent complaint by such an "outsider," see Leland Ryken, *The Word of God in English: Criteria for Excellence in Bible Translation* (Wheaton, Ill.: Crossway, 2002). Note the appendix (ibid., 295-327) by C. John Collins, who has more of an "insider's" understanding of the issues.

CONTINUED DEVELOPMENT

Linguistically-based translation theory has continued to develop since Nida wrote in 1964.[62] Analysis of propositional relations and discourse has enriched the early model.[63] Translators like Ernst-August Gutt have explicitly criticized over-simple approaches to meaning that characterized the early days of translation theory.[64] Kenneth L. Pike early recognized the complexity of interlocking between form and meaning, and the embedding of language meaning in a larger human context.[65] Textlinguistics emphasizes the role of a full discourse, including paragraphs and larger cohesive structures, rather than confining attention only to individual sentences in isolation.[66]

And above all, better translators have always known that translation is an art; Nida's and others' technical tools are only properly used as one dimension in the process of trying to do justice to total meaning.[67]

All this is good news. But the dangers of reductionism remain as long as linguists and translation theorists experience pressure from the prestige of scientific rigor. Rigor is possible in linguistics and in translation when we isolate a sufficiently small piece of language, or one dimension of language, and temporarily ignore the residue that does not cleanly fit into a formalized model. Such models offer insights, but the clumsy, the doltish, and the arrogant can still misuse them.

---

[62] See, for example, the extensive bibliography at http://www.ethnologue.com/bibliography.asp.

[63] John Beekman and John Callow, *Translating the Word of God: With Scripture and Topical Indexes* (Grand Rapids, Mich.: Zondervan, 1974), especially 267-342; Kathleen Callow, *Discourse Considerations in Translating the Word of God* (Grand Rapids, Mich.: Zondervan, 1974). For a framework that acknowledges still more dimensions of meaning, see Vern S. Poythress, "A Framework for Discourse Analysis: The Components of a Discourse, from a Tagmemic Viewpoint," *Semiotica* 38-3/4 (1982): 277-298; Vern S. Poythress, "Hierarchy in Discourse Analysis: A Revision of Tagmemics," *Semiotica* 40-1/2 (1982): 107-137.

[64] Ernst-August Gutt, *Relevance Theory: A Guide to Successful Communication in Translation* (Dallas: Summer Institute of Linguistics, 1992); *Translation and Relevance: Cognition and Context* (Oxford/Cambridge: Blackwell, 1991).

[65] Kenneth L. Pike, *Language in Relation to a Unified Theory of the Structure of Human Behavior* (The Hague/Paris: Mouton, 1967), especially 62-63; I illustrate in Vern S. Poythress, "Gender and Generic Pronouns in English Bible Translation," in *Language and Life: Essays in Memory of Kenneth L. Pike*, Mary Ruth Wise, Thomas N. Headland, and Ruth M. Brend, eds. (Dallas: SIL International and The University of Texas at Arlington, 2003), 371-380.

[66] See, in particular, Robert E. Longacre, *The Grammar of Discourse*, 2nd ed. (New York: Plenum, 1996); Robert E. Longacre, "Holistic Textlinguistics," SIL, 2003 (available online at http://www.sil.org/silewp/2003/silewp2003-004.pdf).

[67] But Nichols, "Translating," demonstrates that in practice translators adhering to the "dynamic equivalence" approach associated with Eugene Nida have too seldom risen above the limitations of a reductionistic theory of meaning.

5

REVELATION VERSUS RHETORIC:

Paul and the First-century Corinthian Fad

BRUCE WINTER

SENECA THE YOUNGER (4 B.C.–A.D. 65), like Paul his contemporary, was subjected to criticism for the way in which he wrote his letters. This came as something of a surprise for the former, who was a noted Stoic philosopher and a Roman senator known primarily in New Testament circles because he was the brother of Gallio, the proconsul of Achaea and judge in the case of the Jews *versus* Paul in Corinth (Acts 18:12-17). His education along with that of his brother had been carefully supervised in Rome by his very ambitious father, Seneca the Elder. Seneca the Younger had been the personal tutor of Nero prior to his becoming emperor not long before his seventeenth birthday. Seneca the Younger became a highly influential political figure during that Principate, acquiring the accolade of the *amicus principis* of Nero. It was in that period he wrote to his friend, Lucilius, now the procurator of Sicily, who had complained about the style of the correspondence he had been receiving from Seneca while in Sicily. In a highly revealing response to that criticism, he explained the significance of his having written in the way he did in his correspondence with Lucilius:

> You have been complaining that my letters to you are rather carelessly written. Now who talks carefully unless he also desires to talk affectedly. I prefer that my letters should be just what my conversa-

tion would be if you and I were sitting in one another's company or taking walks together,—spontaneous and easy; for my letters have nothing strained or artificial about them. . . . That person has fulfilled his promise who is the same person both when you see him and when you hear him. We shall not fail to see what sort of man he is and how large a man he is, if only he is one and the same. Our words should not aim to please but to help. Let it [eloquence] be of such a kind that it displays the facts rather than itself. It and other arts are wholly concerned with cleverness; but our business here is the soul.[1]

Seneca had already written many letters in this style to Lucilius, whom he says "should be content to have conveyed my feelings to you without having either embellished them or lowered their dignity." He further reveals that he was opposed to 'affectation' in letters,[2] and asserts that there was nothing "strained or artificial" about his communications. Lucilius was to be reassured that he could take Seneca at his word as their relationship was based on integrity. His letters reflected his sincerity because they revealed his real thoughts. He went on to say, "I should like to convince you entirely of one fact—that I feel whatever I say, that I not only feel it, but am wedded to it." He was a man of conviction, as his literary remains reveal. He further explains his approach in correspondence with Lucilius by way of contrast with the construed display of the orators with their "rhetorical delivery" (ὑπόκρισις). He states that, "I should not stamp my foot, or toss my arms about, or raise my voice," for he leaves "that sort of thing to the orators [the rhetoricans]."[3]

     Letter writing in the Roman world was a highly significant activity, for it took cognizance of the social connection between the author and the intended recipient. It was an expression of established relationships built, as they all were, around rank and status. A letter-writer's current relationship with recipients also influenced the tone in which he wrote as well as the way in which he constructed it, and all the more so in the

---

[1] Seneca the Younger, "On the Diseases of the Soul," *Letter to Lucilius*, lxxv, 1.
[2] As the editor of the Loeb translation noted, Seneca's choice of the term *putidum*, which indicated "affectation," was also used by Cicero, *De Oratio* iii. 41.
[3] For an examination of the preoccupation by orators with ὑπόκρισις that is based primarily on an examination of Philodemus, see my "Philodemus and Paul on Rhetorical Delivery (ὑπόκρισις)," in J. T. Fitzgerald, D. Obbink, and G. S. Holland, eds., *Philodemus and the New Testament World*, Supplement to Novum Testamentum CXI (Leiden: Brill, 2004) 323-342.

Second Sophistic which had burst forth into bloom in the time of Claudius.[4]

This helps explain the reasoning behind the complaint to Seneca, who was not following the contemporary fad. He was highly capable of framing letters in the grand style of rhetoric, for he had been educated in rhetoric in Rome. There is evidence that his father took him to hear and learn from the leading orators of the day. On his part, Lucilius, *in absentia* from Rome, was concerned about what the lack of care being shown in the way the letters were framed actually meant. They were not in the epistolary form, and he misinterpreted this as something of a regression in their relationship. Seneca, however, felt their relationship was of such intimacy, which was reflected in his relaxed style, that it came as a surprise to him that this had not been apparent to Lucilius.

Seneca helpfully reveals the options that were open to Paul as a letter-writer, an issue highly relevant to our subject of revelation and rhetoric in Paul. His letters had likewise come under scrutiny from some of his recipients, namely the Corinthian Christians and, in particular, his detractors. We do have important evidence that 1 Corinthians, along with other letters to Corinthian Christians, drew comments from some of their recipients (2 Cor. 10:9-11). Paul's response in the face of that provides some clues as to how he had meant his letters to be received and read, as well as his response to the other criticisms by his Corinthian detractors.

Paul's communications to the churches under his apostolic jurisdiction have been judged by some New Testament scholars to be epistles that were structured along the canons of rhetorical handbooks. The issue is not an unimportant one to address, because there has been a scholarly revival in recent years of reading 1 Corinthians and other of Paul's letters through the grid of epistolary rhetoric.

Ancient historians who specialize in the literature of the late Republic and Early Empire and work outside the New Testament guild have expressed doubts that rhetorical structures are appropriate grids for reading New Testament letters and would not classify them as "epis-

---

[4] For agreement that the beginning of the Second Sophistic was the Julio-Claudian period, based on my gathering of primary literary and non-literary sources in Alexandria and Corinth, see the foreword by G. W. Bowersock in my *Philo and Paul Among the Sophists, Alexandrian and Corinthian Responses to a Julio-Claudian Movement*, 2nd ed. (Grand Rapids, Mich.: Eerdmans, 2002), ix.

tles." After examining the epistolary style of three ancient letter writers from the early Second Sophistic period—Alciphron, Aelian and Philostratus—Rosenmeyer observed that their "letters were master-pieces of rhetorical display, paeans to classicism" which aimed to demonstrate "the prowess of their authors in rhetoric and Attic Greek."[5] As Lucilius noted, the ones from Seneca did not have that hallmark of the grand style so popular and so expected in that time; nor, it will be suggested, did Paul's.

The purpose of this contribution is to examine whether the nature of the relationship with the recipients of 1 Corinthians was such that Paul's approach in his communications with the Corinthian Christians was not dissimilar to that of Seneca with Lucilius, adopting something of a non-epistolary writing style in his interactive, informal style. Was it as if Paul were in "conversation" with them, "sitting" in their company or "taking walks" together, to use Seneca's description of his own rela-tionship with Lucilius? Did he write in the rhetorical tradition that was disdained by Seneca, as some scholars have suggested he did? Or did he, like his contemporary, abandon such a form because it was inappropri-ate given the familial relationship between himself and the Christian community and the nature of his letters to them?

Even though he was a cultural "outsider," I will suggest that Paul could have competed with the best of them when it came to the use of rhetoric, in much the same way Favorinus used it so effectively in the same city some fifty years later.[6] Strategically, there was certainly every reason for him to have done so, for that had become *the* fad among the educated in his day, who valued the grand style—and none more so than the inhabitants of the proud Roman colony of Corinth.[7]

Does Paul, like his contemporary Seneca the Younger, provide any clues as to where he stood on the register of rhetoric in his verbal and written compositions to friends? We have important information in 1 Corinthians 2 on the topic of revelation versus rhetoric, although it is not immediately obvious on an initial reading that in 2:1-5 Paul dealt

[5] P. A. Rosenmeyer, *Ancient Epistolary Fictions: The Letter in Greek Literature* (Cambridge: Cambridge University Press, 2001), section 4, at 343.
[6] See my "Toppling of Favorinus and Paul by the Corinthians," in J. T. Fitzgerald, T. H. Olbricht, and L. M. White, eds., *Early Christianity and Classical Culture: Comparative Studies in Honor of Abraham J. Malherbe* (Leiden: Brill, 2003), 291-306; and my *Philo and Paul Among the Sophists*, 246-252.
[7] Dio Chrysostom, *Or.* 8:9.

with rhetoric or that 2:6-16 is Paul's clearest declaration in any of his letters on the issue of revelation.

This chapter suggests that Paul deliberately did not go down that rhetoric path in spite of the societal pressure of his day to do so. This, of course, has substantial implications for our translation and reading of his letters that we regard from a confessional stance as Scripture.

There are four issues to address to enable us to draw conclusions on revelation versus rhetoric in Paul in the context of the first-century world. These are (I) the relationship between Paul and the recipients of his letters; (II) his self-disclosure as to why he adopted the approach he did with the Corinthian community concerning rhetoric; (III) Paul's claim concerning revelation and the mind of Christ; and (IV) Paul and the "grand style."

I. PAUL AND THE RECIPIENTS

Just as Seneca's letter reveals the nexus between the recipient and his approach, so too does 1 Corinthians. How did Paul address those to whom he wrote? Introductions to letters in the ancient world were important. They were formal and standardized. They might indicate immediately the rank and status of the writer and the recipient by the order in which their names were placed, with the person of higher rank and status taking precedence.[8] Commentators tend to resolve this question by addressing the opening verses of 1 Corinthians 1:1-3, concluding that Paul is following formal letter writing conventions:

> Paul, called by the will of God to be an apostle of Christ Jesus, and our brother Sosthenes, to the church of God that is in Corinth, to those sanctified in Christ Jesus, called to be saints together with all those who in every place call upon the name of our Lord Jesus Christ, both their Lord and ours, grace and peace to you from God our Father and the Lord Jesus Christ (1:1-3).[9]

However, the key as to the relationship between Paul and the recipients is in a particular term of address he used throughout the letter and not

---

[8] R. Coles, "Reports of Proceedings in Papyri," *Papyrologia Bruscelensia* 4 (Brussels, 1966).

[9] Scripture quotations in this chapter are the author's translation.

in judgments made of the standard genre of the opening sentence. By first-century standards Paul used a startling term, "brother," and did so more in 1 Corinthians than in any other letter he wrote. It was invoked in the vocative plural in twenty instances out of thirty-four occurrences in the letter, and in the plural form twenty-seven times. In fact, it was clearly his predominant form of address to the Corinthian Christians.

In Roman law the use of the term beyond sibling relationships had no legitimacy and therefore had no currency in society generally. It was highly improper and illegal to have used it of those who were not siblings either by birth or adoption. Of course the term refers to male and female. One did not write ἀδελφὸς καὶ ἀδελφή, for the former term was understood as inclusive. It was a highly significant one to have used, and its use was backed up by the place in which the early Christian movement chose to meet, i.e., in homes. They could have readily hired halls, as Paul did in Ephesus when debating with non-Christians (Acts 19:9). In first-century culture you met in the setting that expressed who you were and what you were doing, whether the theatre, the *odeon*, the *bouleterion*. In the case of the early Christian movement they chose the home or, more correctly, the meeting room of a home, in which to gather. It reinforced that they were family, brothers and sisters together, and that when they met, they were not defined as others were in the context of Corinth by secular rank and status, but by Jesus' designation, "all of you are brothers" (Matt. 23:8).

The handbooks on rhetoric and the *Progymnasmata* contain no advice as to how you should write to your siblings. Menander Rhetor, while providing important details as to the appropriate forms of address and the protocol that applied in letters, throws no light on how to write to family members.[10] So the handbooks do not provide a *genre*.

Sibling language would have been judged to be out of place in an association setting to describe the reality of the relationship between those who were in it. Later, Tertullian was to record the reaction by outsiders to what they regarded as totally inappropriate:

> Yes, their indignation at us for using among ourselves the name of
> "brothers" must really, I take it, come from nothing but the fact that

---

[10] D. A. Russell and N. G. Wilson, *Menandor Rhetor* (Oxford: Clarendon, 1981).

among them every name of kinship so far as affection goes is false. But we are your brothers, too, by right of descent from one mother, Nature—even if you fall short of being men because you are bad brothers. But how much more fittingly are those who come to know one Father God who have drunk of one Spirit of holiness, who from one womb of common ignorance have come with wonder to the one light of Truth![11]

In keeping with his apologetic technique, Tertullian was initially dismissive of their objection, yet hastens to explain away its starkness by modifying the meaning of the term by using it of common humanity. However he qualifies it by indicating that the pagans were bad examples of this. He goes on to indicate that the term is "much more fittingly" used of those who come to know "one Father God." He is perhaps a little uncomfortable having to explain it to the outsider. Paul is uninhibited in using it of the Corinthians as he is "sitting down" in their company or "taking walks"—to borrow Seneca's phrases—together as he writes to his brothers and sisters on issues about which they have written. In the Julio-Claudian period, he was sailing in uncharted waters, for his letters were written to spiritual siblings and were designed to be read initially in a Christian ἐκκλησία.

II. PAUL AND RHETORIC IN 1 CORINTHIANS 2:1-5

Does Paul discuss the issue of rhetoric? In 2:1 he refers to his *modus operandi* when he arrived in Corinth; this provides a helpful lead. The "entry" of public orators into a city provided the opportunity to proclaim their prowess in this new fad of rhetoric that was sweeping the empire. There were the conventional praise of the virtues of the city, a self-effacing but highly sophisticated boasting about one's achievements, and a presentation oration on the subject nominated from the floor and on which one could declaim either instantly or within twenty-four hours.

On Paul's coming to Corinth he refers specifically to the grand style of rhetoric in 2:1, asserting that in making known "the witness or mystery of God" he did not resort to either rhetoric or wisdom. His phrases refer to superlative rhetoric and to knowledge achieved through learn-

---

[11] Tertullian, *Apology*, 39, 8-9.

ing. It is significant that Paul adds "lofty," referring to the grand style of rhetoric and wisdom. He has already intimated to the Corinthians that his preaching of the cross was not done by means of the "wisdom of rhetoric" (1:17) and then he goes on to parody the concept of rhetoric by referring to the "rhetoric" or "word" of the cross as an absurdity to the perishing (1:18).

Secondly, Paul did not need the topic to be nominated by the audience, for he had predetermined what it was: "Jesus Christ and that crucified" (2:2). In Paul's case there was, in the eyes of the Corinthians, a discrepancy between the grand style of oratory and the great looking orator who possessed rhetorical delivery (i.e., bodily presence and great rhetorical prowess in his speech) and himself. In fact he came in for criticism in 2 Corinthians 10:10 on this very point.

In 1 Corinthians 2:3 there is a reference to his "presence" among them, which he describes as "weakness"—an antonym for "power," which was a synonym for "rhetoric"[12]—"and fear and much trembling," the very antithesis of the stage "presence" (ὑπόκρισις) of the confident virtuoso orator before a first-century audience. They dramatically acted out the oration using "ethos" (ἦθος) and "pathos" (πάθος) but Paul unfolded his presentation in "weakness, and fear and much trembling." Janet Fairweather, in commenting on this verse, states that Paul was "setting standards alien to Greek sophistic by his declaration, i.e., fear *et al*. Humility was uncharacteristic of ancient orators."[13]

Paul's rhetoric (λόγος) and its content (κήρυγμα) were not in the plausible rhetoric of wisdom but in the "demonstrations"—not the use of "demonstration" (ἀπόδειξις) recommended to and used by orators as they crafted their speeches,[14] but that of the Spirit (2:4). His stated reason for abandoning rhetorical demonstrations was so that the Corinthians "faith/proof" would not rest in the wisdom of men but, he emphatically states, in "the power of God," remembering that "power" was a synonym for "rhetoric" and πιστις in rhetoric meant "proof" (2:5). By first-century reckoning Paul had adopted an anti-rhetorical stance and, in doing so, had clearly bucked the latest fad. To the fastid-

---

[12] R. G. Buxton, *Persuasion in Greek Tragedy* (Cambridge: Cambridge University Press, 1982), 10-12, 48-53.

[13] Janet Fairweather, "Galatians and Classical Rhetoric: Part 3," *Tyndale Bulletin* 45, no. 2 (1994): 232.

[14] Aristotle, *Nicomachean Ethics*, 1.iii.

iously demanding Corinthians, ignoring the grand style would have been unthinkable, but in 1 Corinthians 1–4 Paul defends his reasons for it (1:17-31 and 2:1-5) as part of a wider critique of the cult of Christian leadership in Corinth.[15]

In concluding this section on rhetoric it is important to reflect on the fact that Paul has renounced for presentation purposes the conventions of orators and the devices used by its promoters at the time of the flowering of what is known among ancient historians as the Second Sophistic. For him the grand style of the orators and the grand style of oratory were antithetical to the Christian messengers and message. Where was "the debater of this age," i.e., the sophist?[16] God had made the sophist's wisdom look foolish, as he said he would (1:19-20, citing Isa. 29:14). Secular Corinthians would say, "What a great orator," but Paul wanted the Christians there to say, "What a great redeemer," and not "What a great teacher." His *modus operandi* was shaped by the message and not by the contemporary fad.

III. PAUL AND REVELATION IN 1 CORINTHIANS 2:6-16

It is significant that Paul follows this immediately with an antithetical discussion of the wisdom of God, set over against the wisdom of men (2:5). In 2:6 he affirms that we "are speaking" [a present tense] "wisdom, not that of the present age or of its rulers, but" (ἀλλά) he affirms "we are speaking the wisdom of God, the wisdom that was hidden and one that was decreed before the ages for the purpose of the Christian's glorification" (2:7). This self-same wisdom was hidden from the rulers of this age, otherwise they would not have crucified the Lord of glory (2:8). "But" (ἀλλά) again Paul emphatically states, "those things eye has not seen, nor ear heard, nor the heart of man has conceived, . . . to us God has revealed" them—note the emphasis on "us" in the word placement at the beginning of the main sentence—and he has done this "through the Spirit" (2:9-10).

Using an analogy, Paul says that only a person can know his or her own thoughts, and only the Spirit of God can know the thoughts of God (2:11). The Spirit has access to the mind of God (2:12a), and Paul has

---

[15] See my "Paul and Sophistic Conventions," chapter 8 of *Philo and Paul Among the Sophists.*
[16] See my *Philo and Paul Among the Sophists,* 189-192.

not received the spirit of the world but (ἀλλά) the [same] Spirit who is from God, he again asserts. This has been done in order that "we might understand the gifts that God has bestowed" (2:12b). "We are also speaking about them, not in words of wisdom being taught by men, but we are speaking wisdom taught by the Spirit," and it is possible to interpret spiritual gifts to those who possess the Spirit (2:13).

The concluding verses of this section (2:14-16) indicate that the spiritual person has the mind of Christ, clearly something that does not apply to the Christians in Corinth, given their un-Christlike behavior. The citation from Isaiah 40:13, "Who has known the mind of the Lord so as to instruct him?" is followed by the affirmation, "And we ourselves are having the mind of Christ." It is important to note that Paul is being specific about the fact that "we ourselves are having," using a present tense and also placing "we" emphatically at the beginning of the sentence.

Can this refer to the Corinthian Christians?[17] The answer has to be no, for the following verses make it very clear that the Corinthians are still not "spiritual," they are simply Christian babes in arms, indeed "fleshly," behaving in a purely secular fashion, i.e., as ordinary people do (3:1-4). At the beginning of this discussion Paul stated that he is speaking "wisdom" among the mature (2:6), and the Corinthians do not qualify at this juncture. It is suggested that the discussion in 2:6-16 relates to revelation with respect to "us," i.e., Paul and the apostles,[18] and not to his preaching or his gospel.[19]

Paul clearly states that all the discussion about wisdom in 2:6-16 is antithetical to his previous comment about the wisdom of men, which he described in 2:1-5. The latter was admired by the Corinthians inside and outside the church and was delivered with such entertaining rhetorical flourishes and with such panache by the pretentious first-century *vir-*

---

[17] A. R. Hunt, *The Inspired Body: Paul, the Corinthians and Divine Inspiration* (Macon, Ga.: Mercer University Press, 1996), 86, states it does, but does not argue his case.

[18] K. O. Sandnes, *Paul—One of the Prophets?* (Tübingen: J. C. B. Mohr, 1991), 79.

[19] J. Reiling, "Wisdom and Spirit: An Exegesis of 1 Corinthians 2:6-16," in *Text and Testimony: Essays in Honour of A. F. J. Klijn,* T. Baarda, A. Hilhorst, G. P. Luttikhuizer, and A. S. Can der Woude, eds. (Kampen: J. H. Kok, 1988), 200-211, refers to Paul's preaching. Likewise T. W. Gillespie, "Interpreting the Kerygma: Early Christian Prophecy According to 1 Corinthians 2:6-16," in *Early Christian Origins and Christian Beginnings: Essays in Honor of James M. Robinson,* J. Goehring, C. Hedrick, J. Sanders, and H. Betz, eds. (Sonoma: Polebridge, 1990), 156, who suggests that it refers to Paul resuming his discussion of the κηρύσσομεν in 1:23.

tuoso orators. People paid to come to hear them declaim. Parents spent fortunes sending their sons to them to be educated rather than to the philosophers.[20]

The Corinthians clearly do not have the mind of Christ or the mind of God, and that is why they had written to Paul to seek that wisdom on matters he addresses later in the letter (7:1, 25; 8:1; 12:1; 16:1, 12). He praised them for carefully observing his traditions "just as you received them" (11:2). In 1 Corinthians he went on to add substantially to those traditions, giving one hundred and seven commands in 1 Corinthians, of which one hundred are imperatives, five are hortatory subjunctives, and two refer to obligations that were binding on the Corinthians' conscience.[21] If he was speaking simply on his own volition then he was a fraud, laying on the conscience of the Corinthians commands that were simply his own thoughts. He does not differentiate between the binding force of his commands and those of the Lord (7:8-13). Paul, like Seneca, was "wedded to what he said" and, in his case, it was because he was speaking the revealed mind of God and Christ.

IV. PAUL AND HIS CORINTHIAN LETTERS

The issue of the rhetoric in Paul's letters is a critical one, given that much effort continues to be expended on seeking to read Paul's letters through the grid of ancient rhetorical handbooks. Nearly a century ago A. Deissmann argued that Paul was "a non-literary man of the non-literary class in the Imperial Age, but prophet-like rising above his class and surveying the contemporary educated world with the consciousness of superior strength." Deissmann was keen to refute any suggestion that Paul's written communications were "epistles." "The letters of Paul are not literary; they are real letters, not epistles."[22] Of Paul's Greek, M. Thrall concluded that "it is plain that the language of the New Testament as a whole does not reflect the κοινή as it was used by the best

---

[20] Winter, *Philo and Paul Among the Sophists*, 24-30.

[21] For a detailed discussion of this see my "1 Corinthians as Scripture," in *Paul Left Corinth: The Resolution of Conflict and Compromise* (Grand Rapids, Mich.: Eerdmans, forthcoming).

[22] A. Deissmann, *Light from the Ancient East: The New Testament Illustrated by Recent Discovered Texts of the Graeco-Roman World*, English translation (Grand Rapids, Mich.: Baker, 1978), 229, 234. "Only the colour-blindness of pedantry could possibly regard this delightful little letter [Philemon] as a treatise 'On the attitude of Christianity to slavery,'" 234.

educated classes in Hellenistic society, those classes, that is to say, who were well acquainted with the idioms of classical literature."[23]

A decade ago Janet Fairweather, a Cambridge classicist who specialized in rhetoric and was unfamiliar professionally with the New Testament, scrutinized Galatians to see how it read through the rhetorical grid, and what that might tell us about Paul and rhetoric. She had written a major monograph on Seneca the Elder and his rhetorical method, and was well acquainted with the issue of rhetoric in the late Republic and early Empire.[24] She concluded after reading the Pauline *corpus* that he "restricted himself to the level of *koine* in which he writes (a level which earned him criticism by at least some in Corinth), [she] assumes Paul had the ability to write better Greek but *chose* [her italics] not to." She observed that he rejected standard Hellenistic modes of argumentation.[25] She also noted that Paul's style was not an Atticizing one. She cites from a letter the opinion of D. A. Russell, Professor Emeritus of Classical Languages, Oxford University, who observed that Paul's epistolary style was not really "suited to writing" (λεξις γραφική), but "suited to debate" (ἀγωνιστική).[26] These are significant observations from two scholars in ancient history who read Paul's letters from the perspective of their own expertise in rhetoric and ancient literary sources.

If Paul chose not to write in the grand style, did his letter style draw comment as it did in the case of Seneca the Younger? "It says" or "the saying goes: 'On the one hand, his letters are weighty and strong, but on the other, his bodily presence is weak and his speech is of no consequences'" (2 Cor. 10:10). He looked like a weed and spoke like a wimp and therefore by first-century standards he was inadequate as a speaker.

There is no indication who actually made those negative comments about Paul, but 2 Corinthians 10–13 certainly provides some clues. Paul simply refers to "such a one" (ὁ τοιοῦτος) (10:11). He later makes reference to "others" (10:12-15 and 11:13-15). What that person was saying or citing in 10:10 is signaled by the marker "that" (ὅτι) and the verb

---

[23] M. Thrall, *Greek Particles in the New Testament: Linguistic and Exegetical Studies* (Leiden: Brill, 1962), 9.

[24] Janet Fairweather, *Seneca the Elder* (Cambridge: Cambridge University Press, 1981).

[25] Janet Fairweather, "Galatians and Classical Rhetoric: Parts 1 and 2" *Tyndale Bulletin* 45, no. 1 (1994): 1-38; and "Galatians and Classical Rhetoric: Part 3," 45, no. 2 (1994): 213-243, at 236.

[26] Fairweather, "Galatians and Classical Rhetoric: Part 3," 243.

φησίν, which is in the third person singular. It has generally been translated as "they say," but it can be rendered either as "he is saying," "as the saying goes," or "for instance."[27] The absence of any pronouns in 10:10 may indicate that it is a reference to some sort of stock saying or summary of a widely accepted view. What is clear from the context is that Paul's letters were subjected to scrutiny by his Corinthian detractors, because on three occasions in three consecutive sentences the term his "letters" is referred to (10:9-11).

Paul's letters were reported to have been "weighty" or "impressive" (βαρύς) and "strong" (ἰσχυρός). What did that mean with respect to his letters? The immediate context is Paul's discussion concerning his use of authority or power over the congregation, which others saw as being for destructive purposes (10:8). Paul himself records that others accused him of intimidating the Corinthian congregation "through the letters" (διὰ τῶν ἐπιστολῶν), clearly the ones he had written to them (10:8-10a).

Aristotle (*Art of Rhetoric*, III.12.1), in discussing the debating style, drew attention to

> a different style is suitable to each kind of rhetoric. That of written composition is not the same as that of debate; nor, in the case of the latter, is that of public speaking the same as that of the law courts. . . . For the one requires a knowledge of good Greek, while the other prevents the necessity of keeping silent when we wish to communicate something to others. The style of written composition is most precise, that of debate is most suitable for delivery.

He went on to make this important observation:

> When compared, the speeches of writers appear meagre in public debates, while those of the rhetoricians, however well delivered, are amateurish when read . . . hence speeches suited for delivery, when delivery is absent, do not fulfil their proper function and appear silly.

If it is the case that Paul's style is now judged not to be suited to writ-

---

[27] C. K. Barrett, *The Second Epistle to the Corinthians* (London: A. & C. Black, 1973), 260. Cf. Demosthenes, *Against Aristocrates* 89: "For instance (φησίν): 'There shall be the same redress for him as if the person slain were an Athenian.'"

ing, what then are we to make of the comments made about his letters in 2 Corinthians 10:10? The term "vigorous" would certainly have been apposite for a debating mode. What would be made of the description of "weighty"? They certainly conjure up agonistic activity, i.e., athletics and boxing, both of which Paul uses by way of an analogy with respect to his own activities (1 Cor. 9:25-6), and both of which are cited by Aristotle (*Art of Rhetoric*, I.5.14). So the question arises as to whether the comment about his letters is not a pejorative one made by his opponents, in which his style was judged to be inappropriate to the sophisticated culture of letter writing in his day.

T. Morgan has drawn attention to how those trained in rhetoric harnessed it for their own purpose. She demonstrates that "the virtuous and cultured man controls his socio-cultural inferiors. . . . The first is the way in which the ability to speak is constructed among élite writers as a correlate of power; the second is the relationship . . . between the spoken and written forms of right language." Those who were trained in rhetoric saw they had a tool at their disposal that made them superior to those without such an education. "Nowhere is this clearer than in passing references to those who have learnt no rhetoric." They are seen as being unable to act either rationally or effectively. "If, occasionally and despite all ideology to the contrary, they are found speaking, their speech is inadequate and ineffective."[28] Is what is being said here paralleled with Paul's comment that he does want to misuse his authority or to make his recipients fearful (10:8-9)?

Paul refers to "what we ourselves are by means of λόγος through letters (οἶοί ἐσμεν τῷ λόγῳ δι᾽ ἐπιστολῶν), we do when present" (10:11). While the term λόγος is mentioned in a pejorative comment in connection with his rhetorical delivery (10:10b), Paul immediately takes it up in a positive sense in relation to his own letters, "what we are τῷ λόγῳ δι᾽ ἐπιστολῶν" (10:11). He immediately rejects any distinction being made between what he is by λόγος, "through his letters" *in absentia,* and his "labor" or "deed" when present, affirming that any

---

[28] T. Morgan, *Literate Education in the Hellenistic and Roman Worlds* (Cambridge: Cambridge University Press, 1998), 235-236. Quintilian refers to the untrained with the pejorative use of terms such as "barbarians," "peasants," "slaves," "illiterates," "children," and "women." For her sources cited from Quintilian see her notes 153-158.

alleged inconsistency between them on his part is to be emphatically rejected (10:11).

There are cases where λόγος is coupled with ἔγρον which illustrate this dichotomy, and the odious contrast was often implied, according to Merritt, on the basis of his survey of ancient literature: "by fact, not by hearsay I judge" (ἔργῳ κου' λόγῳ),[29] "the false and the seeming—good are those who do all in word, not in fact" (οἱ λόγῳ ἅπαντα ἔργῳ δὲ οὐδεν) or conversely "one should emulate the deed and actions of virtue, not the words (ἔργα καὶ πρήξια . . . οὐ λόγους) "speech is the shadow of action" (λόγος γὰρ ἔργου σκιή). The issue relates not to Paul's speech but to his letters. There was no discrepancy in word or deed on his part (10:11).[30] Seneca the Younger said, in effect, the same when he wrote to Lucilius, "That person has fulfilled his promise who is the same person both when you see him and when you hear him. We shall not fail to see what sort of man he is and how large a man he is, if only he is one and the same."[31]

Neither Paul nor Seneca the Younger aligned themselves with the way that "the debaters of this age" wrote or spoke. Seneca asserted, "Our words should not aim to please but to help. Let it be of such a kind that it displays the facts rather than itself. It and other arts are wholly concerned with cleverness; but our business here is the soul."[32] It was by "the open statement of the truth" that Paul conducted his ministry, and this is reflected in his letters as Scripture that also have to do with the serious business of the soul.

Paul himself indicates that he resorted to plain style, declaring that he has used plain speech, i.e., "frankness," along with "godly sincerity" and not as others did in their letters. The "testimony" of his conscience is this: "we have behaved in the world with frankness and godly sincerity, not by worldly wisdom but by the grace of God." He then explains the implication for his letters: "For we write nothing other than what you can read and also understand" (2 Cor. 1:12).

---

[29] Aeschylus, *Prometheus*, l. 339.
[30] Democritus, *Fragments*, 82, 55, 145. H. W. Merritt, *In Word and Deed: Moral Integrity in Paul*, Emory Studies in Early Christianity (New York: Peter Lang, 1993) widely traverses ancient sources providing good examples of this dichotomy and concludes that what is at stake is Paul's integrity as an apostle in relation to the Corinthian church.
[31] Seneca the Younger, "On the Diseases of the Soul," *Letter to Lucilius*, lxxv, 1.
[32] Ibid.

What does all this mean for the translator? Paul wrote in the plain style of Greek that would have been judged as "unsophisticated" by rhetorical standards and "vulgar" in that it did not reflect classical learning and allusions. He delivered imperatives as to what the Corinthian readership must do. His letter presents no options but contains set menus for the Christian community. While the "grand style" and rhetorical flourishes were the fad of his day and generation, he used plain style in all its simplicity and a word order that gave forcefulness as he conveyed the living oracles of God.[33] That deliberate decision on his part to pursue clarity means that translating his letters demands a comparable plain style such as John Wycliffe and William Tyndale so effectively achieved in their rendering of his letters.[34] It is beholden on their successors to do nothing more and nothing less.

---

[33] Albert Wifstrand, "A Problem Concerning Word Order in the New Testament," in *Epochs and Styles: Selected Writings on the New Testament, Greek Language and Greek Culture in the Post-classical Era* (Tübingen: J. C. B. Mohr, 2005), chapter 4, unfortunately does not focus on Paul but on the remainder of the New Testament corpus.
[34] David Daniell, "The Wyclif ("Lollard") Bible," and "William Tyndale, ?1494-1536," in *The Bible in English: Its History and Influence* (New Haven and London: Yale University Press, 2003), chapters 5 and 9.

GENERAL INDEX

1 John,
    ambiguities in, 99-101
    evocations in, 102
    Greek of, 94-105
    repetition of key words in, 96-99

American Bible Society, 51
Apollinarianism, 38
Aristotle, 116, 147, 148

Barker, K. L., 82
Beekman, John, 69
Blake, William, 85-86
Bloomfield, Leonard, 119-120, 123
"bowels," translated, 24
Brooks, Cleanth, 68
"brother,"
    as used by Jesus, 140
    as used by Paul, 140-141
Bruce, F. F., 100

Callow, John, 69
capital punishment, 32
Carson, D. A., 57, 60
Chomsky, Noam, 120-122, 123, 124
Christ, love of, 67
Christianity Today, 51, 59
componential analysis, 132-133

days, numbering of, 67-68
Deissmann, Adolph, 145
dynamic equivalence translation,
    as interpretation, 50, 62, 66, 67, 72

as modern phenomenon, 63
as "thought for thought," 19, 20-21, 37, 38, 41, 48
as transparent to the modern reader, 75
as used for academic instruction, 48
as used for Christian education, 49
as used for group and personal study, 49
as used for memorization, 49
as used for preaching, 49
basic tenets of, 95
definition of, 20

"elder," as added in translation, 46
essentially literal translation,
    as simple, 62-63
    as transparent to the original text, 75
    as used for teaching, study, preaching, and memorization, 49-50
    as "word-for-word," 19, 20-21, 52, 58, 82, 95
    definition of, 20, 58
    goal of, 65, 83
    or "formal equivalence," 20

"face to face," as missing in translation, 41-42
Fairweather, Janet, 142, 146
Favorinus, 138